PEARSON
Prentice Hall
BUSINESS

Books that make you better

Books that make you better. That make you *be* better, *do* better, *feel* better. Whether you want to upgrade your personal skills or change your job, whether you want to improve your managerial style, become a more powerful communicator, or be stimulated and inspired as you work.

Prentice Hall Business is leading the field with a new breed of skills, careers and development books. Books that are a cut above the mainstream – in topic, content and delivery – with an edge and verve that will make you better, with less effort.

Books that are as sharp and smart as you are.

Prentice Hall Business.
We work harder – so you don't have to.

For more details on products, and to contact us, visit
www.pearsoned.co.uk

How to do a
Great
Job
... and go home
on time

Fergus O'Connell

Harlow, England • London • New York • Boston • San Francisco • Toronto • Sydney • Singapore • Hong Kong
Tokyo • Seoul • Taipei • New Delhi • Cape Town • Madrid • Mexico City • Amsterdam • Munich • Paris • Milan

PEARSON EDUCATION LIMITED

Edinburgh Gate
Harlow CM20 2JE
Tel: +44 (0)1279 623623
Fax: +44 (0)1279 431059
Website: www.pearsoned.co.uk

First published in Great Britain 2005

ISBN-13: 978-0-273-70455-3
ISBN-10: 0-273-70455-9

British Library Cataloguing in Publication Data
A catalogue record for this book is available from the British Library

Library of Congress Cataloging-in-Publication Data
O'Connell, Fergus.
    How to do a great job . . . AND go home on time / Fergus O'Connell.
      p. cm.
    ISBN-13: 978-0-273-70455-3 (alk. paper)
    ISBN-10: 0-273-70455-9 (alk. paper)
      1. Success in business—Handbooks, manuals, etc. 2. Job satisfaction—Handbooks, manuals, etc. I. Title.

HF5386.O25 2005
650.1—dc22   2005050905

10 9 8 7 6 5 4 3 2 1
09 08 07 06 05

Typeset in 10.5pt Iowan by 70
Printed and bound in Great Britain by Bell & Bain Ltd, Glasgow

The Publisher's policy is to use paper manufactured from sustainable forests.

This book is dedicated to
Liam O'Connell, a great salesman and
Christy O'Connell, a great businessman

Contents

CONTENTS

About the author

Fergus O'Connell is one of the world's leading authorities on project management and getting things done in the shortest possible time. The *Sunday Business Post* has described him as having 'more strings to his bow than a Stradivarius'. He has a first in mathematical physics and has worked in information technology, software development and general management.

In 1992, he founded ETP (www.etpint.com), which is now one of the world's leading programme- and project-management companies. His project-management method – structured project management/the ten steps – has influenced a generation of project managers and has been used on some of the world's most prestigious projects, most recently on the Special Olympics 2003. His experience covers projects around the world; he has taught project management in Europe, North America, South America and the Far East.

Fergus is the author of five books:

- *How to Run Successful Projects: The Silver Bullet*, 3rd edn

- *How to Run Successful High-Tech Project-based Organizations*
- *How to Run Successful Projects in Web-time*
- *Simply Brilliant: The Competitive Advantage of Common Sense*, 2nd edn
- *Call the Swallow*

The first of these, sometimes known simply as *The Silver Bullet*, has become both a bestseller and a classic. *Simply Brilliant* – also a bestseller – was runner-up in the W H Smith Book Awards 2002. *Call the Swallow* was shortlisted for the 2002 Kerry Ingredients Irish Fiction Prize and nominated for the Hughes & Hughes/*Sunday Independent* Novel of the Year. His books have been translated into nine languages.

Fergus has written on project management for the *Sunday Business Post, Computer Weekly* and the *Wall Street Journal*. He has lectured on project management at University College Cork, Bentley College, Boston University and the Michael Smurfit Graduate School of Business and on television for the National Technological University.

He has two children and lives with his partner in France.

Acknowledgements

Once again, this book comes to you courtesy of Rachael Stock at Pearson Education. This time Rachael's contribution was way above and beyond the call of duty. Once again, it's hard to imagine a better editor. Once again, lunch is on me, Rachael!

Thanks to Phil Chambers and Andrew Kinsella of the Institute of Business Analysts and Consultants for forcing me to get this stuff together. And thank you to all the people who've attended workshops on this subject and have taught me much of what's here.

I cannot say enough thank-yous to Mark Peplow and Daragh Byrne for reading the second draft of this book and giving me so much useful input.

Finally, thank you to Clare, the love of my life, and not forgetting Suzie.

CHAPTER 1

THE PROMISE OF WORK/LIFE BALANCE

Work/life balance is about more than just getting out the door at 5.00 p.m. every day. This chapter holds out the promise of work/life balance to you. It tells you how the life that you may have only been imagining is actually achievable.

Q.1 You're flat out. Your boss comes in and asks you to do something for her. It's urgent. What's your correct response?

(a) Say yes. You have no choice.

(b) Say no. (Note that this would imply you do have a choice.)

(c) Negotiate. Say I can do this, but then something else will have to give.

(d) Cancel your arrangements for this evening, stay late and get the thing done.

Q.2 The biggest obstacle to people having a work/life balance is:

(a) The culture of the company in which they work.

(b) Their boss.

(c) The industry sector in which they work.

(d) A belief that it's not actually possible to have a work/life balance in this day and age.

Q.3 Your best chance of having a work/life balance is:

(a) Moving to a company where they have work/life balance programmes.

(b) Just moving company. No place could be as bad as where you are at the moment.

(c) Making different choices every day in work.

(d) It's impossible. There is no chance.

Answers

Q.1 (a) 0 points You *do* have a choice. Why that is so is the subject of this book.

     (b) 2 points You could. That would certainly be better than (a).

     (c) 5 points Yep.

     (d) 0 points This is the same answer as (a).

Q.2 (a) 0 points No. Though many people believe that this is so.

     (b) 0 points Nor is it this. Though many people also believe it to be so.

     (c) 0 points Nor this. In my experience, the problem is completely independent of industry sector and whether public or private.

     (d) 5 points Yep. Hit the nail on the head.

Q.3 (a) 2 points Can't hurt.

     (b) 0 points Wrong answer. (And believe me, you'd be surprised.)

     (c) 5 points Yep. Now you're starting to get the hang of it.

     (d) 0 points Wrong. Completely and utterly wrong.

Scores

15 points   A good start. You're thinking the right way.

5–12 points   You're not a complete lost cause.

Fewer than 5 points   Hmmm – you're going to take a bit of work.

Work would be fine – it would be *really* good – if people didn't keep asking us to do things. We could sit at our desks and relax in those nice chairs they bought for us. We could use the phone to talk to our friends and relations. We could send e-mails and stay in touch with those far away. If we were feeling lonely, or particularly gregarious, we could have a meeting.

Instead, of course, people keep asking us to do things. And as if that weren't bad enough, they ask us in a way that makes no sense: 'Here's a job. I'm not too clear what needs to be done – you figure that out. I want it done yesterday. And you have no resources to do it.' It'd be like driving the car into a garage and saying to the mechanic: 'There's something wrong with my car. I want you to fix it in the next 20 minutes and it better only cost 30 euros/pounds/dollars.' Or going to the doctor and saying: 'I don't know what's wrong with me. I want you to diagnose it now. No tests, and I want to be completely fine by Monday.'

It'd be crazy enough for us to say that to the mechanic or the doctor. But imagine how freaked out we'd be if they said, 'Yeah, OK!' In our kinds of work, conversations like this happen routinely.

Many of the things we get asked to do are difficult to do, impossible to do, or well beyond impossible to do. Often we'll show this to the powers that be. We'll build a plan or a schedule and show that what they're asking us to do can't be done; that in order to achieve what they are looking for we should have started six months ago. Or we'll show them that given our workload, there's no way that we could do what they're asking us to do, or not in that time and for that budget. It doesn't matter. They say things like, 'I'm sorry – we just have to do it.' Or, 'Saying no just isn't an option.' Or, 'That's not the culture round here.' Or, 'We want can-do people here.' Or, 'Sure, it's an aggressive schedule, but I'm sure you'll find a way.' Or, 'The problem with you is that you're far too negative.' Or, 'If you don't do it, I'll find somebody who will.' Or, 'You're going to have to learn to be more flexible.' Or much worse things.

And so we try to do these impossible missions.

Sometimes our efforts result in monumental disasters. But sometimes – incredibly – we pull them off. We take something that everybody said was impossible and we manage to get it done.

If we do this, if we manage to pull off an impossible mission, we join a very select club that we call the Magicians' Club. Magicians do exactly as the name suggests. They do magic tricks. They take things that looked as though they couldn't be done and make them happen.

And, in a sense, we can't say enough good things about magicians. They provide an astonishing level of service. They do magic tricks. Imagine you went to an interview and the interviewer asked, 'What do you do?' and you replied, 'I do impossible missions.' Seems to me they'd hand you the contract and say, 'How much do we have to pay you?'

There are other good things we can say about magicians. I think it's true to say that not everybody in the company is a magician. We'd all have to nod our heads on that one. And so, companies should love their magicians. Bring them flowers and champagne. Give them bonuses and stock options and salary rises and company cars and all the rest of it. Love them to death.

But there is a problem with being a magician that we need to talk about. There is a dark secret at the heart of being a magician. It's probably best illustrated by a graph (see Figure 1.1).

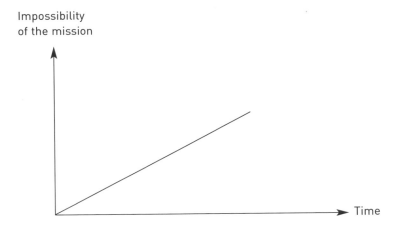

Figure 1.1

On the horizontal axis is time. On the vertical axis is the impossibility of the mission. On the low end of the scale, the mission is only mildly impossible. On the high end, everybody's completely lost the plot. So, as with all magicians, your career starts out on the low end of the scale. You begin by doing low-grade tricks.

So try and imagine now that you're in a theatre. In the front row, just beyond the footlights, you can see all of the people affected by what you do. (We'll call them the 'stakeholders'.) There's your boss, your boss's boss, your team (if you have one), your colleagues and co-workers, your customers and so on. Now, you walk on stage in your magician's costume, and right before their eyes you pull a rabbit from the hat. And the audience goes wild. They're applauding, cheering, whistling, stamping their feet. Your boss is nudging your boss's boss and saying, 'That's my magician. I hired him/her. Isn't he/she wonderful?' Your team are saying, 'He/she led us to victory.' It's a sweet moment. If you've ever had one, and I'm sure you have, you'll know just how sweet it can be.

Now the next time you go on stage, a rabbit from the hat really isn't going to impress anybody. But that's OK. Encouraged by your success, you'll try a bigger animal. Little dogs to begin with. Poodles. And then bigger dogs. German shepherds. And then a very big dog indeed. An Irish wolfhound. And that probably does it with canines. You move on to equines. Mules, donkeys, ponies, racehorses, show-jumpers. Then – relentlessly – giraffes, hippopotamuses, rhinoceroses, elephants. If you stay at this long enough, you'll eventually pull the biggest mammal on Earth from the hat. The blue whale. All 150 tons of it, pulled – excruciatingly – from the hat.

And while most of the stakeholders are still delighted – overwhelmed, indeed, at the scale of your achievement – there are some who aren't quite as perky as they were when all this began. Your team, for example, is exhausted, having just endured another 'death march' project [1]. And for the first time, we notice some stakeholders that we hadn't really paid much attention to before. They're in the second row and they're our husbands, wives, children, lovers, boyfriends, girlfriends, brothers, sisters, parents, pets – those people who love us and like to see us occasionally. They're not looking particularly happy as our magician performances mean that we spend less and less time with them.

You would think that when you'd done the blue whale, you could stop. You would think that the company would put up a little plaque on your office door or cubicle wall. It would say, 'This is Charly's* office. He/she pulled the blue whale from the hat. Tread softly as you walk by.' You would have a sort of honorary retirement, and people would come and gaze in awe at the person who had achieved so much.

Of course, nothing could be further from the truth. If you've done the blue whale, then the stakeholders will just look for a more spectacular trick. Given that there are no bigger mammals to pull from hats, you turn your attention to sawing the lady in half. (I'm assuming you know this

---

* Charly is a character who occurs throughout this book. He can be male or she can be female. Any resemblance to actual characters living or dead is purely coincidental.

trick. There's a large rectangular box, a bit like a big coffin. A woman lies in it. Her head sticks out of a hole at one end and her feet stick out of two holes at the other. The magician takes a saw and saws the box down the centre. Then he separates the two pieces of the box. The woman's head and torso are in one section of the box and they appear to be separated from her legs and feet, which are in the other.)

And so you start sawing ladies in half. And the stakeholders are stunned. They thought they'd seen it all with mammals from hats, but this has brought your magicianship to a whole other level.

Now, one night you go on stage, you put the lady in the box, you start the chainsaw, you saw down the centre of the box and fountains of blood come out everywhere. The trick goes horribly wrong. And it's a terrible moment. It's a terrible, terrible moment. It's particularly terrible for your team, who have worked so hard only to see the whole thing go horribly wrong. It's terrible for the stakeholders. They hadn't been expecting this. And sometimes the retribution can be terrible.

What happens to magicians after that? Well, for a while, they may stay in that organization. They may continue to go on stage. But when they do, the confidence of former times is replaced by terror. You don't know, the stakeholders don't know, the lady in the box doesn't know, what's going to happen when you start to chainsaw. Almost inevitably, the haggard stumbling figure of the burnt-out (for such they are) magician moves on. They go to a new company or organization. They start out low on the scale again, with low-grade tricks, pulling rabbits and other little creatures from hats. But it's only a matter of time before they replay the whole scenario we've already described and end up in the same place.

So, to use a popular word, the dark heart of being a magician is that it is *unsustainable*. It may have some short-term benefits – to the team, your colleagues, your boss, your company, your customers. Long-term, it has no benefits to anybody. But we still return to the point where we started. Magicians are wonderful and we should love them.

But there's a better thing you can do than become a magician.

You can become a Duke of Wellington. Basically, the deal with this man was that he never lost a battle. The level of service he offered to his stakeholders was that when he made a commitment, they could take it to the bank, i.e. the commitment was rock-solid, iron-clad. They could depend 100 per cent on the commitment he had made.

And so – at last, you may say – we come to the contention of this book. You should give up being a magician. Hand back your Magicians' Union card. Say that you're going elsewhere. The Magicians' Union may be select, but it's nowhere near as select as the Duke of Wellington's Union. You can become a person who always delivers on their commitments and meets all their targets. No foul-ups, just predictability, over and over again. This will mean happy stakeholders – your team, your boss, your peers, your colleagues, your customers, your loved ones. You will be hugely respected. No matter what kind of business or industry you're in, this take-it-to-the-bank level of service will be an extraordinary thing. It will be extraordinary for you as an individual, as an employee. It would also be extraordinary if it applied to a whole section, or department or division within a company.

From your point of view, you can do this by working fewer hours. You will be less stressed and enjoy work more. In short, you can have a work/life balance.

It may be that at the moment:

- you no longer look forward to work or enjoy your job – Mondays fill you with dread;

- you are working longer and longer hours;

- you feel you are on a treadmill in work that you can't get off;

- life seems to have become an endless round of work and recovering from work;

- you have less and less time for your life outside work;

- you feel you are not managing your work or time as effectively as you could;

- you feel constantly stressed at work;

- you feel you no longer have a work/life balance.

The evidence is that more and more of you are feeling like this. A report called *Still at Work?* published by the Work Foundation in Britain found that over 6 per cent of male workers and more than 4 per cent of female workers in Ireland now put in more than 60 hours a week; 1.4 million Britons do the same [2]. You've heard of absenteeism, but now we're starting to see the rise of 'presenteeism', where people spend ever-longer hours at their place of work, not because it's more productive but because they think it's expected.

It doesn't have to be like that.

Getting to this new way of working is, first and foremost, a decision – a choice – that we can make. The difference between people who do have a work/life balance and those who don't lies in the difference in their habits. This book is about replacing those bad habits with good habits and becoming a slave to those good habits.

If you are tired of the ways things are, there is an alternative. You are standing at a branch in the road. You don't always have to go down the same road. There is another, less well-trodden path. All you have to do is choose to take it. Or, as Yogi Berra, an American baseball player once said: 'When you come to a fork in the road, take it!'

References

1. Yourdon, Edward (2004). *Death March*. Indianapolis: Prentice Hall PTR.
2. Cowling, Mark (2005). *Still at Work? An Empirical Test of Competing Theories of the Long Hours Culture*. London: The Work Foundation. www.theworkfoundation.com/publications/

CHAPTER 2

FIGURING OUT WHERE YOU ARE AT THE MOMENT

This chapter introduces you to a very important and simple tool called the dance card. It shows you how to use a dance card to calculate how far out of whack your work/life balance is at the moment. This measurement will act as a benchmark against which you can gauge any future improvements.

Q.1   You're a worker in your twenties, thirties, forties or fifties. You work crazy hours and are constantly stressed and consumed with work. You have no life outside work to speak of. What do you think the future holds for you?

(a) Work until you die because of the pension crisis.

(b) You'll eventually be made redundant because your job will be outsourced to a cheaper country.

(c) You'll die young from the stress of it all.

(d) Your remaining years will be years of 'quiet desperation'.

(e) Quite a lot of happiness in your working life. (I've broken with tradition here and included five possible answers because the first four seemed so gloomy.)

Q.2   Similar question to the previous one, except for one change. You're a worker in your twenties, thirties, forties or fifties. You have a life outside work. What do you think the future holds for you?

(a) Work until you die because of the pension crisis.

(b) You'll eventually be made redundant because your job will be outsourced to a cheaper country.

(c) You'll die young from the stress of it all.

(d) Your remaining years will be years of 'quiet desperation'.

(e) Quite a lot of happiness in your working life.

Q.3 Similar question to the previous one, except for one other change. You're a worker in your twenties, thirties, forties or fifties. You have a life outside work. In work, you're regarded highly as a person who always delivers on their commitments. What do you think the future holds for you?

(a) Work until you die because of the pension crisis.

(b) You'll eventually be made redundant because your job will be outsourced to a cheaper country.

(c) You'll die young from the stress of it all.

(d) Your remaining years will be years of 'quiet desperation'.

(e) Quite a lot of happiness in your working life.

Answers

Q.1 (a) 5 points   Maybe. Greater minds than mine say that this is what's going to happen. The good news is that research says you will live longer if you keep on working. (Of course, if you have no life outside work then that's actually bad news!)

(b) 5 points   Possibly. What a bummer to have had no life and then find that that happens to you.

(c) 5 points   Quite likely.

(d) 5 points   Quite likely.

(e) 0 points   Quite unlikely.

Q.2   (a) 5 points   Maybe. Work will be a lot more palat-
                          able though.

         (b) 5 points   Maybe. Do you think that if you work
                          harder, or put in more hours, or are
                          always last to leave, that this will
                          reduce/eliminate the likelihood of
                          this happening? (Dream on!)

         (c) 0 points   You won't.

         (d) 0 points   They won't be.

         (e) 5 points   Yes, I think so.

Q.3   (a) 5 points   Maybe. However, you're more likely to
                          have work, and it's more likely to be
                          interesting work.

         (b) 5 points   Might be. Should be easier for you to
                          find other work though.

         (c) 0 points   Nah! You'll live long. You're probably
                          quite unstressed.

         (d) 0 points   Don't think so.

         (e) 5 points   Very much so, I suspect.

Scores

15 points   Easy to get high marks here.

Other than 15 points   So if you didn't, maybe you should
                       read the questions again. Go and
                       have a beer or a glass of wine. Have
                       a good long think about these
                       things. These are *really* important
                       questions.

The first thing we're going to do is understand the scale of the problem. 'If you can't measure it you can't manage it,' the old saying goes. Here, we'll use a tool called a dance card to see how overworked we are.

Also a note on terminology. I use the word 'project' often in this book. When I use it, it's important that you realize what I'm talking about and that you have the correct picture in your head. Yes, a project may be the construction of the Aswan Dam – something large, involving lots of money and a cast of thousands. This is one end of the spectrum. But equally a project can be something very small and modest, like your boss asking you to investigate a new supplier for pencils. Another word I could have used instead is 'job'.

Dance cards

You may not necessarily have thought of things in this way before, but much of life is a problem in supply and demand. Take money. We don't have enough money (supply) to do all the things we'd like to do (demand). Or we have a business and it is successful – revenue (supply) exceeds costs (demand). Or – heaven forbid – our business is unsuccessful because revenue (supply) is less than costs (demand). Or, thinking about resources, we (as a department, division, organization, company) are trying to do too much with too few people or too little equipment. Or thinking in terms of time, there never seem to be enough hours in the day (supply) to do all the things we want to do, have to do or have committed to do (demand).

A dance card is a way of investigating *time* from a supply-and-demand point of view. Just to get it out of the way, the term 'dance card' is a reference to those more genteel days where, when ladies went to dances, they had dance cards showing the (fixed number of) dances that were available that night. Then, if a gentleman wanted to dance with a lady, they wrote their name against a particular dance – a waltz or a polka or whatever. Thus, that time slot was booked and then could not be booked by anybody else. (I hasten to add that I don't remember those days myself! I've merely seen them in movies and read about them in books.)

I hope you can see the analogy. You have a certain amount of time (or time slots) available every day, every week, every month, every year. In work, at home or wherever, certain of those slots get booked by other people – your boss, your customer, people who work for you, your children, your wife, husband, boyfriend, girlfriend and so on. Given that in general there will be more demand on your time than you will be able to satisfy, how can you ensure that you put time into the right things? The dance card, which actually has several uses, is a tool for doing just that.

Figure 2.1 shows an example of a dance card for a six-month period, although dance cards can be for any period of time. (I think you'll agree that it looks suspiciously like a spreadsheet.)

	JOB	NE	ED	6 Mo Total	Jan	Feb	Mar	Apr	May	Jun
	TOTAL DAYS AVAILABLE:	120			20	20	20	20	20	20
1	Client A project	72	days	72	12	12	12	12	12	12
2	Client B project	24	days	24	8	8	4	4	0	0
3	Client C project	10	days	10	0	0	0	2	4	4
4	Selling	2	dpw	48	8	8	8	8	8	8
5	E-mail / Inbox / Admin	1.25	dpw	30	5	5	5	5	5	5
6	Holidays	10	days	10						10
	TOTAL DAYS WORK TO DO:	194		194	33.0	33.0	29.0	31.0	29.0	39.0
	dpw = days per week									
	Assumes 20 days in a month and 4 weeks in a month									

Figure 2.1 Dance card

The column headed 'Job' lists all of the things that the owner of the dance card is involved in. The next two columns indicate how much work is estimated to go into these things over the period under investigation. Days per month (dpm), days per week (dpw), hours per day or just plain days are all good ways of calculating how much work needs to be done. The remaining columns show how this time will be spread out over the period under investigation – in this case, six months. There are two other items of interest. The top row shows how many days are available per month and the total number of days available (120) over the period. (Note that rather than trying to allow for the different numbers of working days in different countries, we have assumed that every month consists of 20 days. You could adjust this up or down for your own situation. For example, in Europe, December is definitely not 20 working days in most companies.) The other item of interest is the total of all the work that this dance card owner has to do – in this example, 194 days.

In the example, then, the owner of this dance card has an overload of more than 50 per cent, i.e. over 50 per cent more work to do than time available to do it.

Dance cards can be calculated over any period of time and can use both work and non-work tasks as you choose. My own philosophy tends to be (a) have a dance card per month and (b) focus on the work-related tasks and reduce these to manageable proportions.

The dance card in Figure 2.1 was for a person who does a mixture of projects – which take reasonably predictable amounts of time – and other kinds of work. However, dance cards can also be used for people whose work is very unpredictable. If your job is like that, then the best thing to do is to record what actually happens in, say, a particular week or over several weeks and then use this as your start point. Figure 2.2 shows a dance card for such a job, with actual time spent in a given week.

		Total hours	8 Mon	8 Tue	8 Wed	8 Thu	8 Fri	0 Sat	0 Sun	40
1	Phone calls	9	9.25	2.25	2.50	3.00	1.00	0.50	0.00	0.00	
2	Admin		7.50	1.75	0.50	0.75	1.50	3.00	0.00	0.00	
3	Status report to boss		1.00					1.00			
4	Running office		4.75	1.00	0.50	1.00	1.00	1.25	0.00	0.00	
5	Overseeing staff		6.25	2.00	1.00	1.00	1.25	1.00	0.00	0.00	
6	E-mail; timesheets; petty cash; stock; phone		5.25	1.00	1.25	0.75	0.75	1.50	0.00	0.00	
7	Interruptions		7.50	1.00	0.50	2.50	2.00	1.50	0.00	0.00	
8	Meetings		6.25	0.00	0.75	1.50	3.00	1.00	0.00	0.00	
9	Bringing work home		6.00		3.00				0.00	3.00	
			53.75	9.00	10.00	10.50	10.50	10.75	0.00	3.00	
	OVERLOAD	34%									

Figure 2.2 Dance card

Drawing up your own dance card

Here's how to draw up your own dance card:

1. Decide what period you want to look at. I suggest that

you pick something in the range of four to eight weeks for this initial dance card. This means that you can cover whatever remains of the current month and a complete calendar month (next month).

2. Make a list of all the projects (if any) you are involved in over the period in question. List any project that:

- starts during this period
- ends during this period
- starts and ends during this period
- runs through this period (see Figure 2.3)

Figure 2.3 Projects

and put these into the 'Job' column of your dance card (see Figure 2.4).

		TOTAL DAYS AVAILABLE:	30			5	5	5	5	5	5	
		JOB	NE	ED	Total time	Week 1	Week 2	Week 3	Week 4	Week 5	Week 6	
	1											
	2											
	3											
	4											
	5											
	6											
		TOTAL DAYS WORK TO DO:				0.0	0.0	0.0	0.0	0.0	0.0		
		Assumes the period being looked at is 6 weeks											

Figure 2.4 Blank dance card

3. Now add 'business as usual'-type projects to your list. Things like:

    - e-mail/inbox

    - meetings/conference calls (not related to any particular project)

    - training (either you're being trained or giving the training)

    - vacation

    - trips (you're going somewhere)

    - visits (somebody's coming to you).

    These aren't projects in the conventional sense, but they're going to consume some of your time over the period.

4. Finally, add one more thing. Let's call it 'New stuff'. It may be that in your job, nothing will change over the period being looked at. (I believe there are such jobs – it's just that I've never come across one.) However, it's probably more likely that new things will come in over the period being looked at. The line item 'New things' will allow for those. This is the equivalent of having contingency available.

5. Now try to figure out how much of your time will go into each of these items over the period being looked at. Hours per day, days per week or just plain days are all good units to use. Enter these in the next three columns of the dance card so that the total time for each item is calculated.

6. Add up the 'Total time' column. This tells you how much work needs to be done over the given period.

7. The total number of weeks (six in the example in Figure 2.3) multiplied by five (days per week) minus any public holidays gives the total amount of time available over the same period.

8. Finally, for completeness, you can fill out the cells of the dance card to see what time occurs in what week. This will let you know whether you're going to have particularly difficult weeks.

9. Record what actually happens. I cannot emphasize this enough. This is the best way to find out where your time is going, and – as we have said – for very unpredictable jobs, it is really the only way.

Interpreting dance cards

I've been looking at dance cards for about 15 years now. Some or all of the following issues almost always emerge when somebody draws up a dance card.

- In more than 90 per cent of cases, people tend to be overloaded.

- The general level of overload has been increasing steadily over the past ten years.

- An overload of up to 50 per cent, i.e. 45 days work to do in a 30-day period, is so routine as to be boring.

- An overload of around 100 per cent is not uncommon. I tend to find it in a third to a half of those dance cards that I see. You know the expression, 'doing the work of two men'. That's what an overload level of 100 per cent represents.

- The biggest level of overload I've ever seen was 310 per cent. This was achieved by somebody on one of my project-management courses – even though it has to be said he spent most of the course outside the door taking calls on one or other of his mobile phones.

- When people see a high level of overload, they have a tendency to think that what is going on is the following: 'I've got a bit of a backlog now (because of end of year is approaching or I'm just back from holidays or whatever), but once I clear this I'll be out on the prairies and running free.' They tend to think that if they could look at their dance card for, say, a particular calendar month a year from now, they would see 20 or so virginal days. In fact, this is not the case. Most people have already given away days (i.e. booked time) way off into the future. Things like e-mail, meetings and some of the other business-as-usual items are the more obvious examples of 'bookings' that have already been made.

- If people are in an overload situation, there are only four things they can do to fix it:

  → Not do certain things at all, or delegate them.

  → Move certain things out beyond the period being looked at.

➜ Work more hours* (or get more done in the hours you do work).

➜ Reduce the quality of what they do. People rarely choose this, but it will happen anyway if you are in an overload situation.

• If somebody is in an overload situation, it will tend only to get worse. It will certainly not get better without some kind of intervention.

So here is your starting point. You may have been surprised by your dance card. Or you may not. Maybe it just confirms what you suspected all along. But if you are unhappy with it, then the chapters that follow will show you how to get it to a level you're comfortable with. In the process, you will end up doing a better job and spending less time in work.

---

* And, as we'll see later in the book, this is not really a solution. Short bursts of extra hours to meet a target or a deadline – no problem. But extended overtime, i.e. long hours of working over long periods of time, gives you less productivity than if you had just worked a 40-hour week.

CHAPTER 3

TAKING THE FIRST STEP

This chapter gives your first taste of the 'cure'. It checks to see whether you have the stomach for what lies ahead.

Q.1 To be highly regarded in your company, you need to:

(a) Work longer hours than anybody else.

(b) Achieve more than anybody else.

(c) Tell it like it is.

(d) Suck up to the boss.

Q.2 You work in a small high-tech company. Everybody from the CEO/founder down works long (i.e. crazy) hours and nobody has a life. If you don't do the same, what will happen?

(a) You'll feel guilty.

(b) You'll get fired.

(c) Your career advancement will be curtailed drastically.

(d) You'll be regarded as a pariah.

Same scenario as the preceding one. You work in a small high-tech company. Everybody from the CEO/founder down works long (i.e. crazy) hours, and nobody has a life. If you want to have a life, which of the following would be the most likely to

understand *precisely* what your boss wants you

adequate resources to do the job.

to the boss.

it is.

Answers

Q.1 (a) 0 points   Maybe some companies are like this, but it's not what you should be chasing after.

      (b) 5 points   Yes, this would do it.

      (c) 3 points   This is also good.

      (d) 0 points   Lots of people do it, but it's not the right answer.

Q.2 (a) 5 points   Probably. Guilt is a powerful (and useless) emotion [1]. We talk about how to deal with it in Chapter 9.

      (b) 1 point   Maybe, though I feel this is most unlikely. Certainly, I've never heard of it.

      (c) 3 points   Possibly.

      (d) 3 points   Possibly.

Q.3 (a) 5 points   Yes.

      (b) 5 points   Yes – and coupled with (a) you'd be unstoppable and have a life.

      (c) 0 points   Wouldn't work with this kind of boss.

      (d) 3 points   Wouldn't do it by itself, but it would certainly help.

Scores

15 points   Good – this is clear thinking. Now the only question is 'How?'

| 2–14 points | I know what you're thinking. You're thinking this is all very well, but how do I actually *do* these things. Stay tuned. That's what the rest of this chapter and much of the rest of the book is about. |
| 1 point | This means you answered (b) in Question 2 and scored 0 in the other two questions. I think you're wrong on all counts. |

Exercise 1

Assuming you're in an overload situation where demand (work to be done) exceeds supply (time available to do the work), here's what I want you to do:

1. Figure out how to lose one day's worth of demand. I don't care how you do it as long as it's legal. When you've figured it out, write what you're going to do in the box below.

How I'm going to lose one day's worth of work from my dance card

---

2. Go into work and do exactly that, i.e. lose that day's worth of demand. Write what happened in this box. Pay particular attention to how people reacted. Were they positive or negative? Maybe different people reacted in different ways. Maybe there was no reaction. How did you feel?

> What actually happened when I tried to lose one day's worth of work from my dance card

3. Knowing what you know now, are there other ways in which you could have lost the day? Write them down here.

> Other ways to lose one day's worth of work from my dance card

What follows is a by no means exhaustive list of ways you could have done this. But don't read on until you've filled in the three boxes on the previous pages.

Ways to lose some demand from your dance card

- Delegate. The job gets done and you don't do it. Could anything be more attractive? If you do choose to delegate, be sure you do it properly, i.e. let it go and just check on its completion. Also, don't think that just because you're not a boss or don't have people reporting to you or a large team to call on that delegation isn't an option for you. Delegation is an option for everybody. You can delegate stuff to your boss (how attractive is that?), you can delegate to your peers, or there may be others around the place who can do the job for you. Obviously it won't always be an option, but don't rule it out without having at least thought about it.

- Even better than this – if you could manage it – would have been to train somebody else to do the particular job. Then it stays delegated, resulting in a permanent reduction for you. Could anything be more attractive? Yes, this could!

- You could possibly get training that would enable you to do your job better, i.e. quicker and more efficiently.

- Prioritize – and then don't do the bottom thing on your list. And just so we're all clear, can we say what we mean by prioritization? Some people talk in terms of having four priority-one things to do, seven priority-two things and 79 (or whatever) priority-three things to do. That's not prioritization. Prioritization is where you say: 'If I could only do one thing, what would it be?' That's your priority-one item. Then you take the remaining list and say: 'If I could do only one thing, what would it be?' That becomes your priority-two item, and so on.

Rewards and treats

This is going to be the best part of each chapter. Here is where you will get your reward for having carried out the exercise of that chapter. Obviously, you only qualify for the rewards and treats if you do the exercise successfully. Here's this chapter's treat:

You've saved a day – a day's work that you don't now have to do. Presumably if you had had this work to do, you would have done it some night or weekend. You'd have stayed late or brought home work. So now you're entitled to a night off. Therefore, some evening, leave work at 5 p.m. and do something fun. It can be anything – a night out, an evening with the kids, cooking a proper meal – whatever you like to do. When you've done it, write when you did it and what you did in the box overleaf.

Exercise 1's treat – leave work at 5 p.m. and take a night off

When you did it:

What you did:

References

1. Dyer, Wayne W. (1977). *Your Erroneous Zones*. London: Michael Joseph.

CHAPTER 4

ANOTHER SMALL DOSE

This chapter gives you another small dose. Should be OK if you managed the previous one.

Q.1 If you are overloaded, who's to blame?

(a) You.

(b) Your boss.

(c) The culture of the company

(d) It's just a fact of life in the twenty-first century.

Q.2 Of the four (only) ways of reducing overload that we identified in Chapter 3, which do you feel are open to you?

(a) Not do certain things at all.

(b) Move certain things out beyond the period being looked at.

(c) Work more hours or get more done in the hours you do work.

(d) Reduce the quality of what you do.

Q.3 Referring to the previous question, you may have said that option (a) – 'Not do certain things at all' – was not open to you. If you did, why do you believe this to be so?

(a) Because the work is there, it has to be done.

(b) Because saying 'no' is not an option.

(c) Because if you say 'no', something bad will happen to you.

(d) Because you don't have the guts to say 'no'.

Answers

Q.1 (a) 5 points Yes!

(b) 0 points Nope. It is not your boss's job to control the amount of work he or she gives to you. That's *your* job. And even if it was your boss's job, then almost all bosses don't do it. Let's be clear what bosses do do in this regard. Almost all bosses will keep giving you work on the basis that you'll tell them when you're full. If you don't tell them, then – their reasoning goes – you can't be full. (If you were only to take one idea away from this book, then the realization that this is so would be well worth the price of the book.)

(c) 0 points Nah. But it's a convenient excuse.

(d) 0 points As is this.

Q.2 (a) 5 points Yes.

(b) 5 points Yes.

(c) –5/5 points Work more hours, no! Read DeMarco, Chapter 15, for a good discussion of why this is a dumb idea [1]. Get more done in the hours you do work? Yes, of course. This is what this chapter is about. Give yourself -5 if you chose the first answer and 5 for the second. If you chose both, give yourself –5.

(d) 0 points   No. Presumably this isn't in any-
                  body's interest.

Q.3 (a) 0 points   Yes, the work is there. But maybe not
                  all of it has to be done, and even if it
                  does it certainly doesn't all have to be
                  done by you.

(b) 0 points   Saying 'no' is always an option. It's
                  how you go about saying 'no' that's
                  important.

(c) 0 points   An illusion. Most unlikely – particu-
                  larly if you say 'no' in the right way.

(d) 2 points   I gave you the points for your refresh-
                  ing honesty. I agree that saying 'no'
                  can be difficult. We'll be talking about
                  the easiest and most effective way to
                  do it in Chapter 6.

Scores

12 points   Good. You're very much in tune with
                  what we're trying to do.

0–11 points   Yes, it is difficult, but it's not impos-
                  sible.

Fewer than 0 points   You got the *big* question wrong here
                  – as well as being wrong generally.
                  Doing a great job and going home on
                  time is eminently doable, but you
                  need to play your part.

In the exercise in the previous chapter, you chose to reduce the demand side of your supply/demand imbalance. You can also increase the supply side. Working more hours is the most obvious way of doing this. This whole book is devoted to *not* doing that!

However, you can also increase the supply in a more subtle and ingenious way. You can get more done in the time you do work. You can spend your time more effectively. You can get more bang for the buck, as the saying goes. Here's this chapter's exercise.

Exercise 2

1. Figure out one way to get more out of the time you spend in work. When you've figured it out, write down what you're going to do in the box below.

How I'm going to get more out of the time I spend in work

2. Now go into work and implement it. When you've done so, write down what happened in the box overleaf. Pay particular attention to how people reacted. Were they positive or negative? Maybe different people reacted in different ways. Maybe there was no reaction. How did you feel?

> What happened when I tried to get more out of the time
> I spent in work

3. Knowing what you know now, are there any other ways in which you could have got more out of the time you spend in work? Write them down here. (There are lots, so I've left lots of space for them.)

> Other ways to get more out of the time I spend in work

What follows is a by no means exhaustive list of ways you could have done this. But don't read on until you've filled in the three boxes on the previous pages. There really shouldn't be any problem with this exercise. There are lots of ways, and you don't have to be particularly controversial when you implement them. Here's the list:

Ways to get more done in the time you spend in work

- Prioritize the work that you have to do every day. Make a list at the start of each day (or, better still, at the end of the preceding day) and work your way through it.

- Have only one thing to do at any given time, i.e. do one thing at a time and finish it (i.e. close it out completely) before moving on to the next thing. This and the previous method constitute a very powerful pair of actions. With these, you'll no longer waste time dithering over what you're going to do next.

- Go some place where you can get some quiet time. A different location, a conference room, somebody else's office or desk, the cafeteria, another department, another building, some place where people don't expect to find you. Notice that this can include working from home or coming in early. (But then you've got to be sure that you leave early by the same amount of time!) Switch to public transport if that's an option and it will give you quiet time. If this isn't an option, is there any other way in which you can make use of your travel time? If that's not possible, can you reduce your travel time or eliminate it on some days? Can you get more flexible working hours that would be conducive to getting you quiet time?

- Reduce/decline interruptions. Use 'red time' and 'green time'. Green time is when you can be interrupted. During red time, you don't take interruptions. If necessary, put an arrangement in place to cover when you're in red time. If you choose to do this, you have to enforce it. You don't have to be obnoxious about it. If somebody comes along and tries to interrupt during your red time, just say: 'Look, I'm really involved in this problem at the moment (say it even if you don't have a problem). Can I come back to you at eleven (or whenever your red time ends)?' Most people will respect a gentle request like that.

- Deal effectively with time-sucking people. They come in and interrupt you. Invent an imaginary meeting you have to go to, and excuse yourself and walk out of your office or cubicle. Or invent an imaginary deadline that you're working to, and say that, unfortunately, you're going to have to cut the conversation short. Or, if they phone up and you can't get rid of them with the previous tricks, try the following. Begin saying something and with the hand that is not holding the handset hang up the call. It will sound to them like you have been cut off. Take the phone off the hook so that when they call back it's engaged. With mobile phones, the blessing of 'you're breaking up' can also be used to great effect. If they continue to pester over little things that don't matter, then you can also use the techniques in Chapter 6 on saying 'no' and managing expectations to control these people. It's important to remember that you're not at their mercy, that you're not a willing victim. There are things you can do to manage these people and reduce their impact. But you have to take action – you can't just keep bemoaning your lot.

- Make a plan for the day. Last thing before you go home or first thing the next morning, make a prioritized list of what has to be done. By definition, those items near the top of the list have to be done today; those near the bottom are nice-to-haves. Be sure to put some contingency in the plan. By this I mean that if you want to get out at 5 p.m., try to be finished by 4 p.m. Then, if somebody comes along with something 'urgent', you have a good chance of getting it done and still being out by 5 p.m. I call this the 'hot-date scenario' – it's how you would organize your day if you had the hottest date of your life later that evening. Many of the people who have trains/buses to catch at specific times or children to pick up from school do this.

- Realize that there may be a difference between finishing something and getting it done. There may be a point at which you have to say enough is enough. That gets as much of the job done that matters and anything else is window dressing. For a wider discussion of this subject, you could look at Hall [2].

- Reduce interruptions some more. Make yourself 'not available'. Switch off your mobile phone. Set it to 'silent' or 'meeting'. Make better use of out-of-office messages and voicemail. Set phone to 'busy'. Divert your phone to voicemail. Turn off your 'you've got mail' indicator.

- Reduce interruptions still more. Don't be so helpful. Minimize non-work-related contacts. Write an e-mail instead of having a long conversation.

- Be more together regarding meetings:

  → Reduce meetings and meeting times.

  → Decline meetings.

  → Leave meetings when your bit is finished ('Can I do my bit first?').

  → Always have an agenda. An agenda is not a list of things to be done. An agenda is a list of things to be done with the amount of meeting time that is going to be allocated to each.

  → Refuse to go to a meeting that doesn't have an agenda.

  → Start and finish on time.

  → Give people who are late for meetings jobs to do, e.g. write the minutes.

  → Rotate the chairing of meetings.

  → Make sure everyone who's part of the problem being considered attends the meeting.

  → Ensure nobody gets out until the deal is done or the problem is sorted.

  → Have a standing-up meeting.

→ Run more effective meetings, i.e. have rules.

→ Never go to a meeting that has more than three people. (OK, so that's a bit extreme – although I did have somebody on a course once who told me he did exactly that, and he claimed that it improved the quality of his life no end. I suppose what we should say is to aim to keep the number of people at a meeting to a minimum.)

• Save time by streamlining or improving processes. Write FAQs (frequently asked questions) or other useful documentation. Make these things available to others. Conversely, don't reinvent the wheel. Teach people how to do things rather than doing them yourself.

• Know yourself. There may be times when you are 'in the zone' and then it makes sense to keep going. There may be other times when it's hopeless and you really just need to give up and go home. I know myself that if I start feeling sleepy, it's a sure sign that I'm starting to lose it. Then I'm better off either switching to getting lots of trivial, no-brain things out of the way, or – ideally, if I can – just packing it in for the day. (A nap also has a lot to recommend it; I realize this can be difficult in the office, but there's always the bathroom. And I'm not joking.)

• Stop procrastinating and faffing about. Many people work very long hours and come home saying 'I didn't get anything done today' or 'Where did the day (week) go?'. Often, the causes are the ugly sisters of procrastination and faffing about. Procrastination makes you put off doing certain things – particularly unpleasant things. Faffing about causes you to toy with things but never actually sink your teeth into them and say that you're not going home until they're done. Faffing about can also be thought of as engaging in displacement activity. You do something (usually easy or pleasurable) so that you won't have to do something else (which is generally more challenging or unpleasant.)

If the ugly sisters are friends of yours, then you need to deal with them. Decide at the beginning of the day what you need to get done that day. Couple this with offering yourself a reward – you're going to do these particular things and when they're done, you're going home. The clear statement of what has to be done – almost like a checklist – coupled with the vision of walking out into the carpark early with these tasks complete may help to motivate you and stop you from getting sidetracked.

The procrastination may be caused by not knowing how to tackle a job. But if that's the case, just start it. Start somewhere. Begin scratching away at it. In all likelihood, things will start to flow and the way forward will become clear.

Rewards and treats

There now! That wasn't too difficult, was it? If you implemented your idea successfully, that's good. However, to get the reward you need *to implement your idea continuously for 30 days* until it becomes a natural habit – part of the way you normally work. So put in your 30 days. Feel free to implement other ideas, either from the list above or that you thought of yourself. Write down what idea you implemented each day.

Day	What idea(s) I implemented
1	
2	
3	
4	
5	
6	
7	
8	
9	
10	
11	
12	
13	
14	
15	
16	
17	
18	
19	
20	
21	
22	
23	
24	
25	
26	

27

28

29

30

At the end of the 30 days, claim your treat. Spend a little money on yourself any way you want. Maybe don't spend too much at this stage because on subsequent exercises – if you get them done – I'm going to ask you to spend a greater amount on yourself. You know your own budget best and only you can put a value on these exercises and what you gain from them. Write down what you bought and why.

Exercise 2's treat – buy something for yourself

What did you buy?

Why?

You may be the sort of person who doesn't like the monetary reward thing, so here's an alternative that you may find attractive. Make a list of all the things you don't have time to do at the moment. After each chapter, if you've done the exercise it will have freed up some time for you. You can then reward yourself by picking one of these things and doing it.

References

1. DeMarco, Tom (1997). *The Deadline: A Novel About Project Management*. New York: Dorset House Publishing.
2. Hall, Richard (2005). *Success! The Need to Succeed is in Your Genes, the Way to Succeed is in This Book*. London: Prentice Hall.

CHAPTER 5

THE FIRST BIG ONE: PRIORITIZING – KNOWING YOUR OBJECTIVES

Nobody ever got promoted for keeping an empty inbox. Be clear on your objectives and then focus on your priorities. Don't do something that's not in your objectives. To do a great job and leave on time, this is one of the three things you need.

Q.1 How many priorities can you have?

(a) There's no limit.

(b) Around seven.

(c) A handful.

(d) One.

Q.2 Why do people have trouble prioritizing?

(a) Because they haven't agreed with their boss on what's important.

(b) Because their boss hasn't told them what's important.

(c) Because their boss doesn't know what's important.

(d) Because they're not clear how they're being measured.

Q.3 You're already overloaded. Your boss comes along and gives you a new project to do. What does your boss assume in each of the following scenarios?

(a) You say yes.

(b) You put up some resistance but then you say yes.

(c) You resist strenuously. Your boss says: 'We [we!] have no other choice. We have to do it.' You say yes.

(d) You tell your boss you'll make a plan for the project to see what can be done. You then make such a plan. It shows that what he's asking you to do is impossible. You tell him this, take him through the plan and show him why it's impossible. He shrugs and says: 'We have no other choice. We have to do it.' You say yes.

Answers

Q.1 (a) 1 points   OK, sure – the question *is* vague and phrased badly. But it's deliberate and I've given every answer a point for openers to make up for that. So yes, you can have lots of things to do.

  (b) 3 points   But you can only focus . . .

  (c) 3 points   . . . on a handful.

  (d) 5 points   And you can have only one priority-one item at any given time.

Q.2 (a) 5 points   In my view, yes, this is what happens.

  (b) 5 points   And this.

  (c) 3 points   You could also look here.

  (d) 5 points   Yes. This is often true and is allied with (a).

Q.3 (a) 5 points   The project will be done.

  (b) 5 points   The project will be done.

  (c) 5 points   The project will be done.

  (d) 5 points   The project will be done. Why would he or she think anything else?

Scores

15 points	You're very much on the right track here.
11–13 points	And you're not a lost cause.
Under 11 points	You're going to be a tough nut to crack.

My father was a salesman – apparently a great one. There was a story he used to tell that went as follows. Allowing for a certain amount of exaggeration, I can't help feeling that this story was autobiographical on my father's part. He would have dragged it out and larded it with much more detail than I have done here. Also, some of the expressions used in the story have been toned down at the request of the publisher!

The sales manager is going through the department one day and he looks into the salesman's office. The salesman is there, not making phone calls or doing his paperwork or anything else. Rather, he is sitting in his chair with his feet up on the desk, making paper aeroplanes and flying them across the room. There is a small pile of them by the door of the office – evidently he has been at this some time. The sales manager goes in and asks the salesman what the hell he thinks he's doing.

'Ah, bugger off,' comes the off-hand reply.

Nobody has ever spoken to the sales manager like this. Furiously he storms out of the office and goes to find his boss, the area manager. The sales manager explains what has happened, and he and the area manager come down to the salesman's office.

'I believe there's a problem,' begins the area manager.

'No problem,' says the salesman, concentrating on folding a new jet.

'But you told the sales manager to bugger off.'

'I did, and why don't you do that too?'

The area manager is outraged and storms out.

It so happens that the area manager's boss, the regional manager, is visiting that day. The sales manager and the area manager go to find him. They explain what's happened and the three men – sales manager, area manager and regional manager – come down to the salesman's office. When they arrive, they find that the pile of paper jets has grown significantly.

The regional manager says: 'Now you know you can't speak to these gentlemen like you just did. This is a very serious matter.'

Without even looking at him, and launching his latest jet, the salesman says: 'Would you go and take a long walk on a short pier.'

The three men leave the office. The sales manager and the area manager look expectantly at the regional manager to see what he's going to do next.

'How are his figures for the quarter?' asks the regional manager unexpectedly.

The area manager looks at the sales manager.

'Very good,' says the sales manager.

'Met his target?' asks the regional manager.

'Exceeded it. He's way over quota.'

The regional manager turns and starts heading for the door.

'Where are you going?' ask the other two as they scurry after him.

'I'm going to find the seafront. You two can make your own arrangements!'

There is a profound lesson in this story. At the risk of stating the obvious, here's what it is: No matter what our job is, some things in it are inherently more important than others. In a salesperson's case, it's usually very clear. Sales, making targets, reaching quotas. But for many of us, the real purpose of our job can be shrouded in lists of vaguely phrased objectives. The end of the year or the end of the quarter comes and, in the salesperson's case, it's glaringly obvious whether he or she has achieved their objectives. But for many of us, there is all sorts of ambiguity. The result is that the end of the year or quarter can come, our annual or quarterly review can be upon us, and we're in the bizarre situation in which we don't know how we're going to be rated. After a quarter or even a year of working, *we don't know whether we've done a good job!* If you think about it, it's completely bizarre – particularly if you consider all of the systems – management by objectives, 360-degree appraisal systems, key result areas, balanced scorecard and the rest of them – that are slopping around the place.

My own job is to run a small (dozen or so people) consulting and training company. We operate in the high-tech sector. Ever since the dot-com bust, there has been only one imperative for companies like ours – survival. Several of our competitors haven't. In such a climate, I have two clear priorities and everything else can go hang. In order, they are:

1. Keep the current customers happy (existing customers).

2. Find new customers, i.e. sales (new customers).

Now, the second of my objectives is as measurable as that of the salesman in my story. I have a monthly target I must reach. However, the first objective – keep the current customers happy – sounds like one of those make-the-world-a-better-place kinds of objective that pop up all the time in peoples' 'goals and objectives'. So, how do I know whether I'm keeping the current customers happy?

Well, incredible as it may seem, I know because I *ask* them. Before I embark, say, on a day's training, I'll say: 'What would we have to do today for it to be an outstanding use of your time? Not just good, or above average, or yeah, it was OK, but *really* outstanding – so that you'd be looking back in three or six month's time or maybe even longer and saying, "That course was really valuable."'

Yes, I ask customers. Not only that; I check with them – sometimes two or three times a day – that we're doing the business and achieving their objectives.

Now, obviously, the circumstances of my business are different from yours. But other than that, we're in the same situation. Have you ever had a conversation with your boss where you've asked 'How could I do the best possible job for you? What would I have to do over the next three months [or whatever] for you to say that I couldn't have done any better? And not just what would I have to do, but how would we both know? How could it be measured? So that it would be self-evident to both of us that I had cleared the bar?' No? No, I didn't think so.

In my last 'real' job – before I started my own company – I used to *write down* what I was proposing to do over the next three months, six months, year or whatever and run it by my boss. I would write down: 'Here's *precisely* what's going to happen.' It would read like a prediction. I would show it to him and ask him whether it was what he wanted. We would stay at it until he was happy – until there was a prediction that he wanted. I would keep saying: 'So, if all these things were done, then you would regard that as a good performance? That would be the best possible contribution I could make to the company?' When he finally said yes, there was one other thing to be done. That was to prioritize the list. What was the single most important thing that had to be done? And the next? And the next? My boss would try to fudge this, but I was having none of it. I'd say things like: 'If it came to the crunch, which of these would be more important?' 'If you could pick only one, which would it be?' This is usually not as difficult as it sounds. You'd be surprised how often the

1. Existing customers
2. New customers

scenario enables you to get clarity on this. When the list and the prioritization was finalized, that was it – we both knew where we stood.

I had other people affected by my job – other stakeholders. Salespeople, end customers, people in regional offices, people in product development at head office. Once I had agreed the list with my number-one stakeholder – my boss – I would then make the list clear to all the other stake-holders. I mightn't necessarily do this all at the one time. I might wait until some kind of conflict arose, and then I would say something like: 'Yeah, I have no problem with that, but it's the priority Charly [not his real name] has set. Check with him, and if he's happy to change it, then I'll go with whatever the two of you decide.' Often, that was enough to kill the particular thing stone dead. But some-times it did result in changed priorities. And fair enough too – the world is a changing place; we'd expect priorities to change. The list was what I worked to. The list gave clar-ity not just on what I would be doing and when it had to be done by, but where I should expect to put in the bulk of my time. The things on top of the list – the high-priority things – would consume the bulk of my time. The things at the bottom of the list might hardly register at all.

If you haven't had such a conversation with your boss and your other stakeholders, then you need to. That's what the next exercise is about. There's a big treat/reward going with it, because this is a tough exercise – a degree of difficulty harder than the preceding two.

This is a tough exercise for both you and your boss. It's tough because both of you are going to have to come up with ways of measuring your job by output (what you contribute) rather than by input (the hours you work). You have to be able to measure your output in such a way that both of you will know whether the job you have done has been good, bad or indifferent.

Exercise 3

1. Go and have a what's-the-best-possible-job-I-could-do-for-you? conversation, as described above, with your boss. Build a list where every item on the list is

    (a) measurable, by which I mean it'd be completely unambiguous as to whether the thing was done or not done;

    (b) prioritized.

2. Write the list along with the measures and priorities in the box opposite.

Write your list here

Priority   Item   Measure

1.

2.

3.

4.

5.

.

.

.

Rewards and treats

That was a tough one. If you got your list done, prioritized, measurable and agreed, then you've done a mighty piece of work. Give yourself a larger sum than the last time to spend on yourself any way you want. Write down what you bought and why.

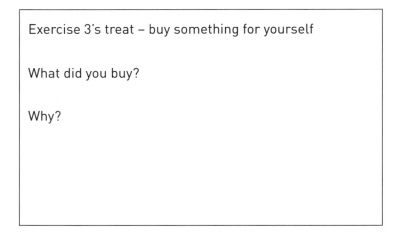

Exercise 3's treat – buy something for yourself

What did you buy?

Why?

(Or as an alternative to this, check out your list of things you don't have time to do. Then, rather than doing one of your low-priority items, do something off your list instead.)

Summary

One of the nice things about teaching courses and then writing books is that on courses, people sometimes say incredibly wise things. If you write them down in your book, it can then sound like you are the wisest person in the world. People sometimes say wise things on my courses. Here are how different people on my courses have described what we have talked about here. It's as good a summary of this most important chapter as you'll get.

'Prioritize your work, i.e. either don't do certain things at all, or let them wait. Use *absolute* priority.'

'Review objectives and refocus/clarify responsibilities.'

'Clarify your role/your department's role.'

'Find out *exactly* what your customers want.'

'Be clear on your objectives and then focus on your priorities.'

'Do important things first.'

'Don't do something that's not in your objectives/job description.'

'Review what you're doing – is it worth it? – are there better things you could be doing?'

The 30-day test

Once you've agreed your objectives with your boss, here's an interesting thing you could try. It both tests the objectives that have been agreed and gets you (and your boss) in the frame of mind for negotiating, the subject of the next chapter.

What you're going to do now that you've agreed your objectives is to show your boss your dance card for the next 30 days, i.e. you're going to show him or her how you're going to spend the next 30 days and how that is going to contribute towards the delivery of your objectives. Here's how you go about it.

1. Make out your dance card for the next 30 days.

2. Go through it with your boss.

3. Look at the supply and demand and see how realistic what you're proposing to do is. If you're heavily overloaded, then there's a fair chance that some of the things you're proposing to do won't happen.

4. See if you can get your boss to (a) see this and (b) do something reasonable about it. See if you can get a final agreed (by both parties) dance card that has reasonable supply–demand balance.

5. Now go off and do what you have to do.

6. Don't be too downhearted if you fail. We will give the wherewithal to succeed in these negotiations in the next chapter.

CHAPTER 6

THE SECOND BIG ONE: NEGOTIATING ONE THING – SAYING NO

If you've stayed with it this far, you've done well. This chapter contains the toughest exercise so far. The reward is big but so is what you have to do. To do a great job and leave on time, this is the second thing you need.

Q.1 A harassed project manager comes to her boss, and says: 'We're due to start the system testing three months from today. Remember that our plan called for two extra test engineers for the system-testing phase? Well, I just wanted to remind you of that now so that human resources have plenty of time to find the two guys.' The boss says: 'But you know we're not going to be able to do that now. There's a hiring freeze on.' The project manager pauses, thinks, looks like she's about to say something, but finally just mumbles 'OK' and walks out. What has the boss heard?

(a) The project is going to be delayed because of the lack of the test engineers.

(b) The project manager is going away to redo the plan and come back with alternatives.

(c) The project will come in on time.

(d) There is no change to the project schedule.

Q.2 Same scenario as before, but instead of saying 'OK' and walking out, the project manager says that she'll have to go away and 'see what that will do to the schedule'. The project manager does that and comes back. She shows the boss every conceivable alternative and says that – best case – there'll be a two-month slip in the project end date. The boss says that that's completely unacceptable and that the project will 'just have to be done [to the original date]'. 'There must be a way,' the boss says. The project manager says 'OK' and walks out. What has the boss heard?

(a) There's a two-month slip in the project.
(b) There must be other alternatives so that the project manager will somehow find a way.
(c) The project will come in on time.
(d) There is no change to the project schedule.

Q.3 Same scenario as in Question 2. This time, though, instead of saying: 'OK', the project manager stands there and says to her boss, 'Well, in that case, you've got a problem' (with a slight emphasis on the 'you'). What has the boss heard?

(a) There could actually be a problem on this project.
(b) Maybe he and the project manager better look again at the alternatives.
(c) The project may not come in on time.
(d) There may well be a change to the project schedule.

Answers

Q.1 (a) 0 points   No. Where did it say that? No, it's not implied. It's not implied at all.

(b) 0 points   No. That's not implied either.

(c) 5 points   Yes. Magician at work!

(d) 5 points   Yes, the boss has heard no bad news about the project. His magician project manager is somehow –

miraculously – going to make this supply–demand problem come right. (Presumably by sweating her existing resources, which as we've already said is a daft and counterproductive idea.)

Q.2 (a) 0 points   No. He hardly heard this at all. Even if he did, he certainly doesn't believe it.

      (b) 5 points   Yes. He heard this.

      (c) 5 points   And this.

      (d) 5 points   And this.

Q.3 (a) 5 points   Yes.

      (b) 5 points   Yes.

      (c) 5 points   Yes.

      (d) 5 points   Yes.

Scores

15 points   There were lots of points going begging here.

Fewer than 15 points   I think it's really important that you scored 15 here. There are only two possible outcomes from such meetings with the boss. Either they heard you or they didn't. Either they accept there's a problem or there isn't. Going in to such a meeting or situation, you have to be clear what you want the boss to hear and then you have to make damn sure – and I mean damn sure – that they hear it. If you are conflicted or ambiguous about the message you are carrying, they'll be more than happy to take the path of least resistance. Don't make it easy for them! Such situations become your problem because you choose to make them your problem. You always have the (much more attractive) choice of telling your boss that *you* can help them sort out *their* problem.

There's a saying 'The customer is always right.' There's another saying 'He who pays the piper calls the tune.' Taken at their most general, these basically say that whoever is paying the bill – customer (external 'real' customer or internal customer), employer, boss – is entitled to get whatever they ask for.

Now, in most normal businesses – and we've mentioned some of them previously – mechanics in garages, doctors, builders, electricians, plumbers, florists, you name it – this is taken to mean that the customer (and remember that this could be – and often is – your boss) says what they want, the specialist does an evaluation, gives a diagnosis and states what they will do when and for how much. The customer can then decide whether they want to give their business to that person or not. If the customer chooses to go with that particular person, the customer is then further entitled to have the what delivered when for the how much.

In our kinds of business – I suppose you could generally call them high-tech industries or knowledge industries – this principle has taken on a different, very mutated meaning. In our business, we take 'The customer is always right' to mean 'The customer is entitled to expect miracles.' Not only that, but, as we described in Chapter 1, we often deliver miracles.

Let's get one thing very clear. If you don't agree with this, you better stop reading now and throw the book away. *Customers (and we're very much including bosses here) are not entitled to expect miracles.* They are entitled to the same things that other (normal) businesses offer, i.e.

1. Customer says what they want.

2. Specialist does an evaluation.

3. Specialist gives a diagnosis.

4. Specialist states what they will do when and for how much.

5. Customer decides.

6. Specialist delivers the what when for the how much.

The last point is the most crucial. The customer may wince at having to pay over, say, £200 for new brake pads. But ultimately he or she wants to know that when they drive the car away it will actually stop when they want it to. The customer is not entitled to expect miracles. Nossir, not at all. *But the customer is entitled to always know how he or she stands.* When the specialist (that's you) makes a commitment to the customer – external 'real' customer or internal customer, employer, boss – that customer is entitled to know that they can rely on the commitment, that they can take it to the bank.

That's all. Not miracles. Just reliability. Always. Every time.

If you can offer this as an employee to your boss, then you would be something of a rarity – somebody who always delivers on their commitments. And if your group or department or company could offer this to its customers, then it would be an extraordinary level of service. It would be a real unique selling point.

There are two things we need to explore to enable us to do all of this. The first is to talk about setting and managing expectations. The second is to discuss what's often referred to loosely as: 'learning to say no'. Let's take them in turn.

Setting and managing expectations

Setting and managing expectations is about ensuring that your customer – external 'real' customer, internal customer, employer, boss – always knows where they stand. The key to success here is to develop the ability to look at things from your customer's point of view and to ensure that he or she sees things from yours. (This idea gets a chapter to itself in *Simply Brilliant* [1].)

For instance, you get an e-mail from a customer. It's going to require full and extensive feedback. Because it came by e-mail there's a fair chance that they expect an almost instantaneous response. But it's going to require significant legwork on your part. So what do you do? Sending back a wall of silence until you get round to doing it isn't managing setting and managing expectations properly. Sending them a 'holding' e-mail straight away saying 'Here is when you can expect a response' is.

Or somebody fails to do their part properly and then asks, 'Where's your part?' Look at it from their point of view. They believe they have done a complete job and are now waiting for you. You need to correct this misapprehension of theirs. Point out to them – politely, of course – how what they have done is lacking. Show them how you will now have to make up for what they have not done. Finally, make them realize how all this additional work will require time (obviously) and, as a result, this is when they can expect whatever it is to happen.

Same with the customer who wants too much. Are they being reasonable or are they asking for too much? Well, if you take the dictum that the customer is always right, then they are allowed to ask for whatever they want. That is their right. However, *your* right then is to point out to them the implications of what they have asked for. If they ask for something small and modest, then that will take a certain amount of time. If they ask for something colossal and unreasonable, then your best way to deal with that is to say: 'Sure, I can do that. But here are the implications of that in terms of time [and, quite possibly, money].' They can then decide what they want to do.

This technique also enables you to not appear obstructive, inflexible or picky about what is and isn't part of your job description. With this technique, you are always willing to do things. But by pointing out the implications of a particular path that the customer is choosing, you often end up not having to say 'no' at all. They do the saying 'no' for you by not choosing that particular path.

You may be starting to worry as to what all of this will do to your career progression. If you start doing a great job and going home on time, will that be it with regard to promotion or career advancement? Will the people who go up the ladder and get the furthest be the ones who do everything? If this is true, then do CEOs work the longest days?

Well, you can decide for yourself, but that is not how the world seems to me. The ones who progress furthest are the ones who do the important things, the things that are really going to make a difference. That's what this book is all about. They do the important things and they manage their workload. (We'll see more techniques for doing the latter in Chapter 7.) Some cynics may say that these people also manage their image, but I'm not sure I necessarily agree with that. Yes, such people may manage their image, but you could argue that if they're doing the important things, if they really are doing a great job, then image and reputation will take care of themselves.

CEOs *don't* work the longest days. The people who go up the ladder are not the ones beavering away on every last little thing. The people who go up the ladder are the people who understand how they can best make an outstanding contribution, and then make it.

There is a great case to be made that saying 'yes' all the time is not at all good for your career prospects. It seems to me that it implies (a) you don't have enough to do, or (b) you're really bad at managing your time (because you always end up staying late due to your workload), or (c) you're just a doormat and so not suited to positions of greater authority or responsibility.

Learning to say 'no'

This skill is actually negotiating. Or, to be precise and clear, it's about when something is handed to you, you don't just agree to it on the basis that the customer is always right, i.e. the customer is entitled to expect miracles. Rather, you go through the steps we outlined above:

1. Customer says what they want.

2. Specialist does an evaluation.

3. Specialist gives a diagnosis.

4. Specialist states what they will do when and for how much.

5. Customer decides.

6. Specialist delivers the what when for the how much.

In the 'Customer decides' step, you stop yourself from making an unreasonable commitment to the customer. That's what 'saying no', or negotiation, will mean for us here.

There are plenty of ways to lose this negotiation. If you decide you're going to win by the force of your personality – either by arguing to the bitter end or schmoozing – you will lose it. If you try to have it with somebody who is more senior than you, then if you don't do what we say below, you will lose it. If you try to have it in a selling-type situation, where you are the one who is selling, so that – essentially – they have money that you want, you will lose it – unless you do what we say below.

The only place you can be guaranteed to win this negotiation is by using the facts. And happily, if you use the facts and stick to your guns, then you can't actually lose the negotiation. This is particularly true when the customer is your boss.

To use the facts, all you do is follow the process that we've already described:

1. *Customer says what they want:* Whether it's the most modest of requests or a large set-piece project or anything in between, this is what customers (and especially bosses) ask you to do – they ask you to do stuff.

2. *Specialist does an evaluation:* You do an evaluation to understand how long it will take and how much work is involved. For modest requests, this could be a back-of-the-envelope calculation or it could even be done in your head (though something written is always intrinsically better). For large set-piece projects, this could involve a large-scale planning and estimating exercise.

3. *Specialist gives a diagnosis:* Based on your evaluation, you size up the situation and identify the alternatives. You are also clear what alternatives are *not* available, i.e. are not possible.

4. *Specialist states what they will do when and for how much:* You state the alternatives to the customer.

5. *Customer decides:* He or she picks one of the alternatives. They are allowed to work with you to explore other alternatives or variations of the alternatives you offered. They are not allowed to pick, i.e. you stop them from picking impossible alternatives. (Bosses are particularly prone to this and need to be stopped.)

6. *Specialist delivers the what when for the how much:* And finally, and most importantly, you deliver on whatever commitment you agreed with the customer.

This is all pretty simple and self-evident, you may say. However, there are a few places where you can go wrong and we need to talk about them.

You get suckered into saying 'Yes'

You get suckered into saying 'Yes' like this: Somebody, e.g. your boss, comes scampering over to you and says something like 'Customer's on the phone now and needs an answer to this straight away. Can we do it?' And you say, 'Yes.' Or somebody gives you a little project and says: 'This is pretty straightforward and, by the way, I need it by the end of the week.' And you say 'Yes.' Or somebody gives you a project and says: 'This is already behind schedule. We should have started it weeks ago. We don't have time to plan it now, we just have to do it.' And you say 'Yes.'

If you want to protect yourself against this, make it a rule to *never* say 'Yes.' *Always* look for that piece of time, be it large or small as required, to do the evaluation and diagnosis steps described above.

You get the estimates wrong such that your commitment can't be met

Hmmm, big problem. You need to learn to plan more real istically and estimate more accurately. Do this by buildir lots of detail into plans and recording estimated vers actual for tasks/projects. If you're interested primaril how long something will take then you're intereste knowing for each task its duration or elapsed tir you're interested primarily in how much someth going to cost, then you're interested in the work o that goes into each task. Try and avoid underest which *everyone* has a tendency to do. Always h contingency in the plan. I've put a little crash estimation at the end of this chapter, which should serve to get you started. However, estimation is a big subject in its own right. Go on a good course – there are lots of bad ones out there – or buy a book. I have written a couple and they're listed at the end of this chapter [2, 3].

You back down because the pressure you get to agree is, or becomes, intolerable

We've said that stakeholders are entitled to know where they stand. Basically, stakeholders are entitled to an honest relationship with you. If you agree to something that you know to be impossible – irrespective of whether a magician-type performance would make it happen – essentially you start out your relationship with your stakeholders by telling them a big fat lie. Big fat lies are not the recipe for any relationship, and they're certainly not the recipe for happy relationships with stakeholders.

pressure becomes intolerable, you'll be safe if you
th the facts. Sooner or later, the people applying the
vill have to back down in the face of reality.

n't have a choice in this regard. You may be
he idea of karma. There is 'stuff' in each of
we don't deal with it, will just keep coming up until we do. Pressure to accept
's a bit like that. If you don't deal with
en the thing is given to you, you'll
s that's created at the end. If you
oject, it'll just come back again
t one, and so on.

Finally, if the pressure really is intolerable, there is a way you can deal with it, which, in certain circumstances, can have certain advantages. It goes like this:

The powers that be are leaning on you to agree to an impossible mission. You, armed with your facts, are resisting. Eventually, you say this: 'Look, the best evidence we have is that what you're asking me to do is impossible. You must see that it would be wrong of me to commit to this. I can't and won't commit to it. However, here's what I will do. I'll take the thing and run with it for a while and see what pans out versus what my plan is saying. If it all starts to run ahead of schedule, then maybe you guys are right – it can be done. On the other hand, if it runs like I have said, then it can't be done.'

They will agree to this.

Now it's important to realize that what they heard was not what you said. What you said was very clear. But what they heard was that their magician was back on the case. This is the phase of the project where they are engaging in denial.

Now, what you do next is very important. Because they have not heard what you said, you need to say it again. And again. And again. Until they do hear it. You do this as follows.

Let's say a period of time has passed and it's clear that your plan is actually very accurate and that it's looking increasingly likely that what they're asking for is impossible. Now, you need to start reminding them of that fact. In memos.

At the water cooler. When you walk into your boss's office and conspiratorially close the door, saying, 'We need to talk about this problem you [very important word] have with the X project.'

What will happen next is a period of irrational behaviour (on their part), where, once again, they try to get you to commit to the impossible. But at this stage, you're even stronger, because now you have evidence that your plan is accurate – something you didn't have when they first leaned on you. If you just stick to your guns, they will move into the period known as waking up and smelling the coffee. And then you're on hand with your plan and specialist knowledge of this project (you do realize, don't you, that you're actually the world's number-one authority on this project?) to help them out of the mess they made for themselves.

Exercise 4

1. The next request that comes your way, do what we've said above, i.e.

    (1) *Customer says what they want:* They say what they want us to do.

    (2) *Specialist does an evaluation:* You do an evaluation to understand how long it will take and how much work is involved.

    (3) *Specialist gives a diagnosis:* Based on our evaluation, you size up the situation and identify the alternatives. You are also clear about what alternatives are *not* available, i.e. are not possible.

(4) *Specialist states what they will do when and for how much:* You state the alternatives to the customer.

(5) *Customer decides:* He or she picks one of the alternatives. They are allowed to work with us to explore other alternatives or variations of the alternatives we offered. They are not allowed to pick, i.e. you stop them from picking impossible alternatives.

(6) *Specialist delivers the what when for the how much:* And finally, and most importantly, you deliver on whatever commitment you agreed with the customer.

2. Now do it nine more times.

3. In the box, write down what each request was and how you dealt with it and tick whether you accepted or didn't accept an impossible mission. (I've filled out a few lines of a sample one below just to give you the idea.)

Write down

Request and how you dealt with it	Accepted	Didn't accept an impossible mission
1.		
2.		
3.		
4.		
5.		
6.		
7.		
8.		
9.		
10.		

Write down

Request and how you dealt with it	Accepted	Didn't accept an impossible mission
1. 'Urgent' request at 5 p.m. to stay late and sort something something out for sales. Told them the earliest I could get to it was tomorrow morning. They accepted it grumpily.		x
2. Handed project with 'an aggressive schedule'. Told that there was no negotiation on this one – that we'd just have to do it. Told them where they could put it.		x
3. Big guns came down about the project with the aggressive schedule. Got a pep talk from the big cheese about how I was the only one who could do it and what it meant on my CV. Told him the alternatives same as I told the others. Impasse continues.		x
4. Got the works about my 'attitude' and about being 'inflexible'. Responded by saying I wouldn't be doing anyone a favour if I agreed, given that I believe what they're asking for is impossible. Reminded them of what is possible.		x
5. Reason prevails!		x
6. And so on.		
7.		
8.		
9.		
10.		

Rewards and treats

That was a tough one. And the grading of your perform-ance is even tougher. If you got ten out ten on 'Didn't accept an impossible mission', then give yourself a greater amount than the last time to spend on yourself any way you want. If you didn't get ten out of ten, I'm afraid there's no treat for you. What you can do, however, is have another go and try to get your perfect ten.

Write down what you bought and why.

Exercise 4's treat – buy something for yourself

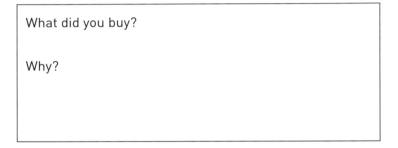

What did you buy?

Why?

Alternatively, do something off your list of things you never have time for. You'll have definitely saved time as a result of this exercise.

Summary

Here's how people on courses have summarized what's in this chapter:

Deflect *some* requests, i.e. tell your boss you're at satu-ration point. (See what happens when you do.)

Do less by saying 'no' positively, i.e. using facts/show them the evidence of how you're fixed.

Stop saying yes to everything you're given – always negotiate.

Revise/decline deadlines. Make people aware of consequences – 'If I take this, I won't be able to do that.'

Redistribute work – 'I'm full.'

Estimation

The problem with doing estimation is that you have to predict the future, something nobody can do with 100 per cent certainty. The best you can hope for here is that the error in your prediction will be as small as possible.

There are two things you can do to help yourself. One is that you can record what happened on previous projects – how long particular tasks took, how much work was involved in them, what they cost – and use this information when you come to plan your next project.

However, in the absence of any comparable information from previous projects, the key to getting the prediction as right as possible is *detail*. By breaking down the work to be done into small elements of detail, then you are less likely to miss vital elements of the project.

One other important point that we need to clarify here is the difference between duration and work.

- *Duration*, sometimes also called elapsed time, is *how long* a particular job is going to take. It is measured in the normal units of time – hours, days, months, and so on. The duration of a football match, for example, is 90 minutes.

- *Work*, sometimes called effort, is how much work is involved in a particular job. It is measured in units like person-days, person-hours, person-years, and so on. The work in a football match, if we count two teams of 11, a referee, two linesmen and a fourth official is 26 multiplied by 90 minutes, i.e. 39 person-hours.

Durations are important because they enable us to figure out *how long* all or part of a project will take. Efforts are important because they enable us to figure out *how much* all or part of a project will cost. To do estimation, carry out the following:

1. Involve the people who will do the project in figuring out the list of jobs. If they're not available, get somebody to help you. The worst thing you can do is do this by yourself.

2. Identify the big pieces of work to be done in the project, the bits that get you from the start to the end.

3. Within each of these big pieces of work, identify the detailed jobs that have to be done.

4. Break down everything such that each job you identify is between one and five days' duration or one to five person-days of work.

5. Be as specific and concrete as possible, i.e. rather than saying 'requirements gathering' say 'Charly meets with the IT people for two days to explain requirements.'

6. Where you don't know something, make an assumption. See the example below for an illustration of this.

7. Store all the jobs in a work-breakdown structure, or WBS, i.e. show the project as being made up of the big pieces of work, which in turn are made up of the smaller pieces. Once again, see the example for an illustration.

Here's a possible piece of WBS related to the user-testing of an IT system.

Project X

```
1 Requirements
  . . .
2 Design
  . . .
3 Build the system
  . . .
4 IT test the system
  . . .
5 Users test the system
```

5.1 First test run	3 days	[The 3 days is an assumption]
5.2 IT fix the errors	2 days	[So is the 2 days]
5.3 Second test run	3 days	[Assume you test everything again]
5.4 IT fix the errors	1 day	[Assuming fewer errors found]
5.4 Final test run	3 days	[And assuming no errors will be found]*

---

* This is obviously simplified. In reality there could be (many) more testing cycles.

References

1. O'Connell, Fergus (2004). *Simply Brilliant: The Competitive Advantage of Common Sense*, 2nd edn. London: Financial Times Prentice Hall.
2. O'Connell, Fergus (2001). *How To Run Successful Projects: The Silver Bullet*, 3rd edn. London: Addison-Wesley.
3. O'Connell, Fergus (2000). *How To Run Successful Projects In Webtime*. Boston: Artech House.

CHAPTER 7

THE THIRD BIG ONE: KEEPING IT GOING – DANCE CARDS AGAIN

You've cracked prioritizing, i.e. figuring out what's important and what's not. You've got the hang of saying 'no' so that you only make commitments you can deliver on. You've done what I've asked you to do and collected the rewards/treats. But it's not enough just to do these things as exercises. You need to be doing them *all* the time. This chapter shows you how. It uses that versatile tool, the dance card, again.

Q.1   You want to start doing a great job and going home on time. But there are plenty of things that could derail you from achieving this goal. Here are four possibles. Which of them are real?

(a) Fear of being fired.

(b) Fear of being sidelined/bypassed.

(c) Your customers suffer, i.e. they get a lower level of service.

(d) Your colleagues/workmates suffer, i.e. they have to take up the slack for you.

Q.2   Here are another four things that could derail you. Which of these are real?

(a) A feeling that you don't have the authority to make the change to this new way of working.

(b) A fear that your organization will lose contracts or business.

(c) Fear that some work mightn't get done.

(d) Your own personal fear of trying to execute this change.

Q.3   And here are four more. Which are real?

(a) The business environment changes.

(b) Lack of belief on your part that executing this change is possible.

(c) You're not assertive enough when it comes to the crunch.

(d) You won't know what to do with all your new-found free time.

Answers

Q.1   (a) 0 points   Nope – never heard of it happening. You're doing a great job, i.e. delivering on all your commitments. On what basis could they possibly fire you? Or even want to? And if they were crazy enough to do it anyway, no court in the land would back them up. You could take two years off work on the unfair dismissal settlement you'd get.

        (b) 0 points   Can't see it. You're doing a great job, by which we mean clearing the bar that you and your boss have set. Why would they bypass you? Seems to me that, if anything, it would be the contrary.

        (c) 0 points   A lower level of service. Your customers are getting a level of service where all your commitments to them are being met. That sounds to me like just about the highest level of service there is.

        (d) 1 point   Ah, interesting one this. I've given you one point because the answer to this question will take a bit of space, i.e. more space than we have here in the question-and-answer part of the chapter. It's discussed in full in Chapters 8 and 9, where we look at approval-seeking and guilt. It shouldn't derail you, of course, and we'll say why in Chapters 8 and 9. But you got the point for spotting that we still had work to do on this one.

Q.2   (a)   0 points   You're actually the only one who has this authority.

(b)   0 points   Because you always deliver on your commitments? Yeah, sure that makes total sense.

(c)   5 points   Some work *won't* get done, silly! That's the whole point. But it doesn't matter, because it'll be the unimportant stuff. Remember the salesman. Five points here for taking this profound truth on board.

(d)   5 points   Could well be. Change is always scary. And how do you deal with fear? There's only one way. You gotta do the thing that you fear. Read the famous bestseller if you want to know more. [1].

Q.3   (a)   0 points   The business environment changes? It changes to a situation where customers want you *not* to deliver on your commitments. Yeah, right!

(b)   5 points   A very real possibility, I'd say. Well, the book has told you how to do it. It's told you why not doing it is not an option and the price you will pay if you don't. But at the end of the day, you have to provide the final piece of pixie dust. It can't be purchased in a book or on a course.

(c) 5 points   Yes – similar to (b). And the answer is the same as for (b). Also saying things in the right way is important, i.e. using the facts.

(d) 0 points   Oh, come on! Learn to cook, learn a language, learn a musical instrument, travel, windsurf, find out who your children are, come and work for me for nothing and I'll take your free time, thanks very much.

Scores

11 points   Good. Very perceptive.
6–10 points   OK. Could do better.
Fewer than 6 points Maybe doing a great job and going home on time isn't for you.

We saw the dance card in Chapter 2. We used it to figure out whether we had an overload problem. Here we're going to use it to (a) fix any overload problem we have and (b) manage our work after that so we don't get into an overload situation again. Here's what you do:

1. Starting with whatever month we're currently in, and working three to six months ahead, set up three to six monthly dance cards. It's 11 November as I write this, so you would set up cards for, say, November, December, January, February, March and April. A typical dance card might look like the one in Figure 7.1.

	TOTAL DAYS AVAILABLE:	22			5	5	5	5	2	
	JOB	NE ED	Total time	Week 1	Week 2	Week 3	Week 4	Week 5	
1									
2									
3									
4									
5									
6									
	TOTAL DAYS WORK TO DO:			0.0	0.0	0.0	0.0	0.0	

Figure 7.1 Monthly dance card

2. Fill out the November card as we described in Chapter 2. Be sure, though, to write in priority order – the priority that you have agreed with your boss – as we described in Chapter 5. Presumably it'll show an overload situation.

3. Now do the same for December through to April. You should see a couple of things happening. The overload should ramp down the further out you go. It may or may not be gone in six months' time, but it should be lower than it is now. The other thing you will see is that you have 'bookings' in your dance card out to April – and beyond, if you care to look that far.

4. To do a great job and go home on time, you want to get the level of overload pretty much at zero, i.e. the 'total

days available' and the 'total days work to do' are pretty much the same each month.

5. You have two choices as to how to deal with whatever overload you currently have. You can suck it up, taking the view that you've made your bed so you'll lie in it. In this scenario, you say you'll work through the level of overload you have, i.e. magician your way through it. Your other choice is to say no; whether I got myself into this situation or not, I want out now. Then you would go to talk to your boss, show him or her the facts (i.e. the dance cards with their supply–demand calculations) and say you need to have something done about it. All the things we said in Chapter 6 would apply, notably the one about not backing down. If you're going to ask for such a meeting, know what you want:

- Opening position: what you'd like.

- Bottom line: what you're prepared to accept.

- What you'll do if you can't get your bottom line. (The tactics are all described in Chapter 6 – especially in the 'Where it can go wrong' piece at the end.)

Either approach is OK in my book.

6. As a result of the point above, you'll have a level of overload that you're going to accept every month until it gets to zero. Let's say it looked something like Figure 7.2.

	Total days available	Total days work to do	
November	22	39	
December	17*	31	
January	20	25	
February	20	21	
March	23	17	
April	21	13	
* Assuming a Western European-type Christmas!			

Figure 7.2

7. Now what happens is that when anything new comes in, it's 'filtered' through your dance card. So in this example, for November through to February, you absolutely can't take on anything new. Either that or if you were to take on something new, it could only be by negotiating (as described in Chapter 6) with the relevant stakeholders that you drop an equivalent (or greater – hey, take advantage of the opportunity!) amount of work.

8. After that – in March – you can take on some new things (six days' worth) in this example. Once your 23 days are full, anything else is by negotiation, once again, with the relevant stakeholders.

9. That's it!

Exercise 5

1. Set up six months' worth of dance cards, as described above.

2. Reduce your overload to zero as described above.

3. When a month ends, close that dance card and open a new one so that you always have a six-month window.

4. If you fall, don't give up – get back on the horse.

5. Claim your reward when your overload hits zero.

6. Fill out the box below before claiming your reward.

> Write down how your life has changed since you carried out this exercise

Rewards and treats

This was the big one. You've become a person who's doing a great job and going home on time. Give yourself a bigger treat than the last time. What you've done is a massive achievement.

Write down what you did and why.

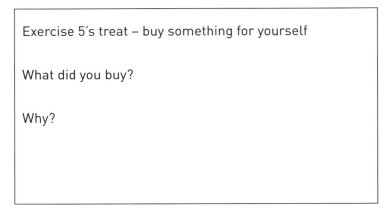

Exercise 5's treat – buy something for yourself

What did you buy?

Why?

Or, instead of doing the monetary thing, use the time to do things you never got to before.

References

1. Jeffers, Susan (1991). *Feel the Fear and Do it Anyway*. London: Arrow Books.

CHAPTER 8

WHAT'S GOING TO STOP YOU? APPROVAL-SEEKING MIGHT

In the questions at the beginning of this and the previous chapter, we talk about some of the things that can derail us from our goal of becoming a person who does a great job and goes home on time. Hopefully we have dealt with some of your issues there. But there are a couple of big issues that arise that need a more thorough discussion. These are approval-seeking and guilt. We talk about them in this and the next chapter.

Q.1   Similar scenario to the questions at the beginning of Chapter 7. You want to start doing a great job and going home on time. But there are plenty of things that could derail you from achieving this goal. Here are four of them. Which of them are real?

(a) Your personal inertia.

(b) The set-up time involved in doing six months' worth of dance cards. You're too busy – you can't afford the time.

(c) You free up all this time, but then the powers that be just give you more work.

(d) Disagreement over your estimates of how long things are going to take or cost.

Q.2   Here are another four. Which of these are real?

(a) The perception of you as a person who is negative all the time, says 'no' and is inflexible.

(b) The company culture is not conducive to this way of working.

(c) You have an unreasonable boss.

(d) New, unexpected things come along and are given to you, which causes the whole process to get derailed

Q.3   Slightly different version of the preceding questions this time. You want to start doing a great job and going home on time. There are heaps of advantages to all of your stakeholders – you, your company, your customers, your colleagues, your boss, your loved ones – if you start doing this. Of the following, which are real?

(a) You can relax a bit and become less stressed.

(b) You'd have more energy.

(c) You'd be more productive, i.e. you'd complete more of the important work.

(d) You'd be a nicer person to work with.

Answers

Q.1 (a) 0 points Sucks to be you! See comments at the beginning of Chapter 7 on pixie dust.

(b) 0 points OK – so why don't you just do what you always do and work extra time to get the dance cards done?

(c) 0 points But you know how to say 'no' by now, don't you? Re-read Chapters 6 and 7 if you're in any doubt about this.

(d) 5 points We talked about this in chapter 6. Another way of dealing with this is to create a history of how long the things you do have taken or have cost in the past. Then, when some genius says 'When I was a lad we could do that in half an hour with one arm tied behind our back,' you can say 'Well, based on the evidence I have, here's how long it's going to take, and the last five times we did it, it took an average of blah and a maximum of blah . . .'

Q.2 (a) 5 points   Possible. To some extent it depends on how you handle the various nego-tiations you have. Gently but firmly is a lot more likely to succeed than aggressively. But more importantly, using the facts, i.e. your dance card, will help make the negotiations eas-ier. Also, the perception of you is the subject of this chapter. Also read Chapter 13 for how such people are usually perceived.

(b) 5 points   With some minuscule exceptions, show me a company culture that is. Changing jobs won't help. You either sort it out where you are or you don't sort it out.

(c) 5 points   Read this chapter on approval-seeking. You'll be providing your boss with a service where you always deliver on your commitments – thus contributing to them delivering on theirs. Read the salesman story again. Read the final chapter of the book. This situation can be tough, but it's not impossible.

(d) 0 points   Nah. Chapters 6 and 7 protect you from this.

Q.3 (a) 5 points   Of course. Prolong your life too.

(b) 5 points   You would. That'd be nice, wouldn't it?

(c) 5 points   You would. That'd be nice too.

(d) 5 points   And with all due respect to you – because I'm sure you're a lovely person to work with – that'd be nice too.

Scores

15 points   The only tricky question here was Question 1 and you got it right.

10 points   Easy to get 10.

5 points   Aren't you great?

Why and how approval-seeking happens

Approval-seeking occurs when you don't trust yourself to make decisions but rather want to check everything out with somebody else first. Independent thinking is not exactly encouraged in our society, so a lot of what we experience as we go through life encourages approval-seeking behaviour. In wanting to be a person who does a great job but still goes home on time, you are proposing to go down the road of independent thinking. Will this get the approval of all of our colleagues, co-workers, bosses, peers, subordinates, team members, customers? Well, what do you think?

These are some of the things we do when we engage in approval-seeking behaviour:

- You don't say 'no' when you should, so that you end up taking on more work than you can realistically do.

- You alter your position on an issue to avoid disapproval. For example, you tell a customer that a certain target is achievable when it isn't.

- You feel depressed or unhappy when you feel people don't approve of you. (Maybe you do go home on time, but you get no pleasure from it because you are worried about what people in work are saying about you, or how they will treat you the next day.)

- You agree when you shouldn't. (Your boss says, 'OK, so, everybody happy with that?' and you fail to voice whatever concerns you have.)

- You get intimidated by people whom you perceive as having some authority or control over you – a boss, a taxi driver, a salesperson and so on.

- You don't want to tell or pass on bad news, e.g. to bosses, to customers, to subordinates.

- You stay late because everybody else stays late. In a more general sense, you subscribe to all aspects of the organization's culture – even those you don't agree with.

What you can do about it

The principal thing you can do about approval-seeking is to realize the profound truth of the saying 'You can please some of the people all of the time and all of the people some of the time, but you can't please all of the people all of the time.' When you express any opinion about anything, no matter how important or trivial, when you take any action, major or minor, there will be people who don't agree with what you've said or done. There may be quite a lot of such people. It's inevitable. It's a part of being alive. It is just as much a part of life as weather, or clothes getting dirty, or summer following winter, or dust under beds.

While we might wish it were not so, it is, and the sooner we get used to the idea, the better. When we say or do anything, plenty of people are going to disapprove.

If you are going to seek everyone else's approval for becoming a person who does a great job and then goes home on time, you're going to be sadly disappointed. For starters, lot of people will be jealous that you have succeeded where they have failed. They may call it 'lack of commitment' on your part, or they may say that you're no longer a 'team player'. They may describe you as selfish and inconsiderate, but basically what you've got here is jealousy, pure and simple. You've cracked it. You do a great job and have a life. They haven't. They toil on in their unceasing labours, the sad things.

The biggest irony of all in approval-seeking behaviour is that the people in the world who gain the most approval are those who *are* independent-minded.

So what can you do to reduce your need for approval-seeking? The following are all possibilities.

- Realize that if someone disapproves of you, the problem is theirs and not yours. Say somebody makes a snide remark about you 'slipping out early'. In the past, you might have tended to be combative – 'What's it to you? I had all my work done.' Or defensive – 'I had to go and pick up my kids' (which might or might not have been true). Or passive-aggressive – gritting your teeth and saying to yourself, 'I'll get him.' Now, instead, you say: 'You had to stay late, did you?' The trick is to turn the comment back on them. Beginning sentences with 'you' instead of 'I' is a masterful way of doing that.

- Take the criticism head-on. Similar to the preceding point, it involves you naming the issue that the other person has placed between you. So, you would say something like: 'Ah, you've noticed I'm trying to get out on time. Yeah, I've done a whole bunch of things to try to help me do that. If you like, I can share some of them with you.'

- Thank them for their observation. Your boss says: 'I see you're not staying back as late as you used to.' You say: 'Yes, you're right. I've been putting a lot of effort into trying to be as efficient as possible.' It defuses the whole thing. If they want to take it up with you again, they'll have to try another approach. And you still have all the other possibilities that we're listing here.

- On the basis that the only way to conquer a fear is to do the thing you're afraid of [2], actively invite disapproval. Deliberately do something that you know will result in disapproval. Then try to stop yourself from getting upset. By courting disapproval, you'll increase your skill at dealing with it.

- Try ignoring disapproval. Just pretend it's not there. Don't use this technique all the time, but rather mix it in with the use of the other techniques on our list here.

- Break the connection between other people's disapproval and your self-esteem. Look at your own track record of achievement. Now disconnect that from the disapproval – the disapproval is their stuff, the achievement is yours.

- Refuse to engage with the people who are sending you the disapproval.

How to say 'no' nicely

When I first came to write this piece of the book, my intention was to give a list of possible ways that this could be done. I would start at the soft end of the spectrum and offer a range of choices between that and the hard end. But then I realized that a method would be a whole lot better than tips and tricks. Here it is.

Let's state the problem. The need for you to say 'no' arises because somebody has an expectation that you are going to be unable to meet. If somebody comes to you with an expectation, then you jointly have a problem. The 'jointly' is important here. They have an expectation; you cannot meet it. Problem. And it's a problem you both have. It's a problem where both points of view have to be treated equally and dealt with. No matter how senior or more powerful they are, both points of view have to be accommodated. A one-sided solution – where typically the weaker party gives in – isn't going to solve the problem.

This is the first important point – focus on the problem and not on the potential personality clash that may be brewing here. An additional benefit of this approach is that if you are the first one to view the scenario as a problem, then you have now taken the upper hand. This is because you are now presenting yourself as the person who will 'help' the other person to fix 'their' problem. Irrespective of how powerful they are, you now have the power, because you're the one who's instigating the solution.

The next thing to do is to understand what their viewpoint really is and, at the same time, to get your viewpoint out on the table. They may have taken up a position, e.g. 'I need this by five o'clock today', but the real question is why do they need it then? What's the urgency? What will happen if they don't get it by then? What's the worst that could happen if they don't? How did this situation come about? The thing is to get all aspects – both yours and theirs – of the problem out in the light, where they can be looked at.

Now generate a bunch of solutions. Look how far away from confrontation we are now. Notice that we are actually well into a whole process of saying 'no' in which the other party is actively engaged! Some solutions may be better for you, some for the other person, but put as many as you can – and certainly not just one – out on the table.

Finally pick one. And if the one that you pick is weighted heavily in favour of the other person, e.g. you do agree to cancel your evening class and stay late, then there should be some major concession to you as part of the deal to make up for that.

If you approach things like this, will people like and respect you? I think so. You'll get a reputation as a caring, problem-solving person who delivers on their commitments. So let's just remind ourselves of the method and then we'll look at some examples. The method is:

1. Separate the people from the problem/focus on the mutual problem.

2. Understand all aspects of the mutual problem.

3. Generate a range of solutions.

4. Pick and implement one.

Example 1

Let's look at some examples. Your airline announces that it's cancelling your flight 'for operational reasons'. The public-address system asks you to go to the desk to rearrange it. You're incandescent with rage, as thoughts of arriving at your hotel early, having a relaxing drink and a nice dinner are evaporating quickly. You join the queue for the desk and eventually arrive at the head of it. The lady smiles nicely and asks how she can help. You freak out. At the end of a tirade, you finish by saying: 'You have to get me to my destination tonight.'

She says: 'Sir, can you see that I can't really help you unless you try to help me?' (She wants you to focus on the problem as she is doing. She has also probably just said no nicely to you – so nicely that you hardly even noticed it.)

You explain where you have to get to and by when. She explains what flights or flight combinations can do that. Now the problem is outlined clearly for both parties. In addition, she has generated a range of possible solutions. You pick one.

Example 2

Your boss – who works at another location – gets his secretary to call you at 5.30 p.m. to say that he wants to talk to you and he'll phone in an hour and a half. The clear implication is that he wants to find you in the office at 7 p.m.

You say: 'I've got to leave now' (i.e. 'no' – said nicely. The choice of words is probably important here. 'Got to' implies that there is some pressing reason, which there may or may not be. Having a nice evening with your family would class as a pressing reason for me. Also, this gets your piece of the mutual problem out on to the table – albeit that you're being nicely vague about what your pressing reason is.) Now you say: 'If Charly really needs to talk to me tonight [now you're trying to find out what his part of the mutual problem is], he could call me at home at 7 p.m. [not your preferred option – but it really could be important that he speak to you] or send me an e-mail, or we could talk in the morning. I'll be in at 8 a.m.' (There: you've nicely generated a range of options. Now let him pick one.)

Example 3

There's a saying that goes 'Your lack of planning is not my emergency.' This is a rather blunt way of saying no – and it can sometimes be very effective. Print it out in large letters on a sheet of paper and hang it up in your office. You'll be pleasantly surprised at the effect it has. However, since the subject of this section is saying 'no' nicely, here's its 'nice' equivalent.

Some genius comes scampering in to you at finishing time and says they have to have this report (or whatever) before you leave. There's two to three hours' work in it.

You say: 'I'm afraid there's no chance of that happening' (i.e. no. Again, the choice of language is important. The implication here is that forces greater than both of you are going to stop this problem from being solved. Also, notice that once again we are focusing on this problem that has arisen.) Next, you say: 'But tell me the story and let me see if there's any way I can help you.' You go on to understand the present urgency and why it could not have been anticipated before now. Then you can offer choices – stay late is clearly an option, but if you chose to dig them out of a hole like this, you would have to insist on something in return. But there are other choices – first thing in the morning, two days' time, or whatever. They then choose from these options.

Example 4

You're very busy and somebody asks you to do something. It's something that you rather like doing and your natural urge is to say yes. However, before you do that, run it through our method and see if that throws up anything.

The mutual problem here is that the other person wants this thing done, you want to do this thing, but you're very busy. So now you need to understand all aspects of the mutual problem. In particular, you need to understand the amount of work involved. Use the estimating ideas in Chapter 6 to help you figure this out. Once you know the amount of work involved, you can then easily pick from options that include (a) accept it, (b) accept it with conditions ('I can't do it now, but I can do it at this time') or (c) say 'no' nicely.

If you would like to find out more about negotiating in this way, pick up a copy of *Getting to Yes* [3]. Based on work done at Harvard University, this little book presents a method called *principled negotiation* or *negotiation on the merits*. The method has as its objective to produce a wise agreement from a negotiation. A wise agreement is defined as 'one which meets the legitimate interest of each side to the extent possible, resolves conflicting interests fairly, is durable and takes community interests into account'.

References

1. Jeffers, Susan (1991). *Feel the Fear and Do it Anyway*. London: Arrow Books.
2. Fisher, Roger, Ury, William & Patton, Bruce (2003). *Getting to Yes: The Secret to Successful Negotiation*. New York: Random House Business Books.

CHAPTER 9

WHAT'S GOING TO STOP YOU? GUILT MIGHT

It's one of the most worthless emotions there is.
We talk about it here.

Q.1 Similar scenario to Question 3 in Chapter 8. You want to start doing a great job and going home on time. There are heaps of advantages to all of your stakeholders – you, your company, your customers, your colleagues, your boss, your loved ones – if you start doing this. Of the following, which are real?

(a) You'll be able to clear whatever backlog you have.

(b) You'll be able to focus and concentrate better.

(c) You'll provide a better level of service to customers. There will be timely delivery. You'll be more focused on customer needs. Ultimately – if you're in the profit-making sector – the company will make more money.

(d) There'll be a better image of you within work.

Q.2 Here are another four. Which of these are real?

(a) You'll do better-quality work.

(b) You'll have a better home life, and you'll actually have a work/life balance.

(c) Your morale will be higher.

(d) It'll be better for your physical wellbeing.

Q.3 Here are another four. Which of these are real?

(a) You'd be setting a good example to others – your boss, your colleagues, your peers, your workmates in particular.

(b) Your work would be more rewarding.

(c) You'd actually have time available to help your colleagues and workmates.

(d) You'd be less of a distraction to your team.

Answers

Q.1   (a) 5 points   You will.

(b) 5 points   Yep.

(c) 5 points   It's all true.

(d) 5 points   And this too.

Q.2   (a) 5 points   You will.

(b) 5 points   You will. Imagine it – a work/life balance!

(c) 5 points   Sure will.

(d) 5 points   *And* you'll live longer.

Q.3   (a) 5 points   You would.

(b) 5 points   It would.

(c) 5 points   If you wanted to use it for that. You could just as easily go home! Or do a mixture of the two. Or get them to do a great job and go home on time.

(d) 5 points   Yep. They'd be like a football team that has a rock-solid goalie. Just there whenever he or she is needed and completely dependable.

Scores

15 points	Lot of advantages, huh? And it's not finished yet – there are a few more in the next chapter.

Whenever I teach workshops on this subject, it isn't long before the 'G' word comes up. Guilt. 'Even if I do a great job,' somebody says, 'If I go home on time, I'll feel guilty.'

Guilt and its twin sister worry are two of the most debilitating emotions in the world today. They're basically the same thing. Guilt is worrying over something that occurred in the past. Worry is feeling guilty about something that may happen in the future.

Mr Dyer is in no doubt about what should be done with them: 'If you have large worry and guilt zones, they must be exterminated, spray-cleaned and sterilized forever.' [1]

The trouble is that guilt and worry seem to have ended up being considered to be good things. If you don't feel guilty, you are a 'bad' person. (I think what's actually happening here is that guilt is being confused with remorse or sorrow for something that happened. You can feel remorse or sorrow for something that happened. You can learn from it. You can resolve to never let it happen again. You can take action to make sure it doesn't happen again. But no amount of guilt is going to undo it.) As for worry, if you don't worry, you're considered 'cold', 'robotic', 'uncaring', an 'android'. Again, worry is different from trying to figure out solutions to a problem. That is a highly creative and, if other people are involved, very caring process. You could hardly be exhibiting more caring behaviour than by racking your brains and using up your energy trying to come up with solutions to problems that affect other people. But worry? What's the point?

Guilt can stop you from becoming a person who does a great job and goes home on time. It can stop you dead! What actually happens is that you think that if you go home on time *you'll feel guilty*. If you're serious about what you're trying to do, you must try to eliminate guilt. Let's see how you might do that.

Why guilt happens

There are two kinds of guilt. The first is guilt left over from our childhood; the second is adult guilt. Both have a common theme: we experience guilt because we feel we have violated some code to which we prescribe. In the first instance, the code has originated from authority figures in our childhood – parents, teachers, religious or other institutional figures. In the second case, it is a code of values that we have built up for ourselves.

Both codes are equally pointless. For leftover guilt, the authority figures are long gone or if not long gone should not have the power over us that they once had. Yet the leftover guilt means that they still exert a power. In the case of adult guilt, the code is a self-imposed standard that we don't actually subscribe to but to which we pay lip service.

Going home on time is a clear example of this. You have authority figures – bosses, peers, subordinates (yes – it's possible!), customers – exerting control over you. In addition, the organization has a (usually unwritten) code that going home on time is slacking. While you don't believe this – if you did, you wouldn't be reading this book – you pay lip service to it. Inwardly fuming that all your important work is done and you can go, you sit at your desk, looking as though you're busy. You go through the motions while outside, life beckons.

What you can do about it

Here are some things you can do to work on reducing your guilt:

- Do something that you know is bound to result in feelings of guilt. (This is the notion that the only way to deal with something you fear is to do it [2].) Leave the office on time. Just get up and walk out the door. Make no excuses. Don't make up any stories, never mind who sees you, just get up and go. Start small. Do it once in a month. Then increase it to once in a week. Then twice a week. Then every second day. Then every day. Reward yourself as you go. Look at how your guilt reduces the more often you do this.

- Tackle the authority figures head-on. If any of the people mentioned previously – bosses, peers, subordinates, customers – makes any reference to your leaving on time, no matter how oblique, indirect or implied, give them the it's-all-about-achievement-not-attendance speech. You don't have to be obnoxious or aggressive. Merely explain how you've done what needs to be done and now you're heading home to the other part of your life. The important thing is to make sure that you never let one of these references go. Always catch them up – they'll soon stop doing it. They may even ask you what the secret of your success is.

- See whether going home on time makes you happy. Yes, subscribing to some sort of unfathomable code can have a certain satisfaction. But ask yourself whether you'd rather be subscribing to a code or doing your job properly and then enjoying life outside work. Answer honestly.

- Reconsider your value system. Which values do you really believe in, and which do you only pretend to accept? Make two lists – the ones you really believe in and the ones you pay lip service to. Be brutal in your choices. Here's an example: in my last 'real' job, I ran a foreign subsidiary of a US software company. In terms of my job, the values I believed in were:

  - providing outstanding service to the customer – we became known as 'the part of X company that worked best';

  - in terms of software-development projects – delivering high-quality products on time and within budget;

  - project schedules should always be realistic; in our subsidiary, we didn't accept impossible missions.

These values were enough for me to do my job properly.

Now the company has a whole bunch of other values. These were things like:

- you weren't really committed to the company if you didn't work very (and I mean *very*) long hours;

- you shouldn't live too far from the office – five or ten minutes' commute was ideal (I commuted an hour and a half each way);

- not accepting impossible missions implied a lack of 'can-do' spirit and, hence, a lack of commitment or lack of 'flexibility';

- going home on time was maybe allowed once in a while but was always commented on ('you went home early yesterday'), and if it became a habit it was frowned on and again seen as a lack of commitment.

I paid lip service to some of these values for a (short) while. Ultimately, I rejected them all, kept my job and was much happier as a result. The company never really accepted my rejection of these values, but that was and remained their problem. I could get along fine and do my job with the values I had.

- Dyer recommends keeping a 'guilt journal' [3]. Write down any things you did that made you feel guilty. What happened, when and with whom? If you keep it religiously for, say, a month, it will give you some useful insights into where your guilt zones are.

References

1. Dyer, Wayne (1977). *Your Erroneous Zones*. London: Michael Joseph.
2. Jeffreys, Susan (1991). *Feel the Fear and Do it Anyway*. London: Arrow Books.
3. Dyer, op. cit.

CHAPTER 10

IF YOU DON'T DO IT, I'LL FIND SOMEBODY WHO WILL

Up until now, we've tended to assume that we're dealing with rational people. With rational people, if you say 'I can only do A or B', the person will say, 'Oh, OK, do B then.' What do we do when we're not dealing with rational people?

Q.1 Your boss says to you: 'If you don't do it I'll find somebody who will.' What options do you have?

(a) Suck it up, i.e. grin and bear it.

(b) Quit.

(c) Suck it up sometimes and resist other times.

(d) Something else.

Q.2 Your boss says to you: 'If you don't do it, I'll find somebody who will.' You choose to always suck it up. Where will this get you?

(a) A happy boss.

(b) A happy you.

(c) An unhappy boss.

(d) An unhappy you.

Q.3 Your boss says to you: 'If you don't do it, I'll find somebody who will.' You choose to quit. Where does this get you?

(a) Unemployed.

(b) A better job.

(c) Able to deal better with these situations if you encounter them again.

(d) Unemployable.

Answers

Q.1 (a) 5 points   Yes. This is one end of the spectrum.

(b) 5 points   And this is the other.

(c) 5 points   And this is what lies in between.

(d) 0 points   You may be right, but *I* can't think of anything else.

Q.2 (a) 3 points   I think this is actually a more complex question than it appears at first sight. You *may* get a happy boss because everything he or she asks you to do is getting done. But see also the answer to (c).

(b) 0 points   Doubt it. For a while, maybe – when you start the job. But eventually, the constant stress, long hours and lack of a life outside work are going to take their toll and you'll end up – sooner or later – deeply unhappy.

(c) 3 points   He or she may be unhappy anyway – the kind of people we're dealing with here often are. Or if you keep accepting stuff, you're eventually going to get to a point where you *do* start messing things up and then he or she won't be happy. Or the resentment building up in you towards them may cause them to be unhappy (with your attitude).

(d) 5 points   You're working harder and harder and messing up more. Hardly the recipe for a happy career (or a happy life), is it?

Q.3 (a) 5 points   Unless you find another job first, then yes.

        (b) 3 points   Possibly.

        (c) 0 points   Doubt it. Look back at Chapter 6 on the subject of karma.

        (d) 3 points   Depends on your circumstances, but yes, possibly.

Scores

15 points   Excellent. Very clear thinking required here.

3–13 points   Yeah, OK.

0 points   This chapter contains some stuff on difficult choices. You need to be thinking clearly – especially before you make such choices.

If you find yourself in the situation we've been describing above, you're faced with difficult choices. As we said, you have three choices:

- Suck it up.
- Quit.
- Suck it up sometimes and resist other times.

There is a fundamental difference between the first two of these options and the third. In the first two, you accept that things are not going to change and make your decision accordingly. In the third, you leave open the possibility that things *could* change. At the risk of stating the obvious, then, it behoves us to try the third one before we move straight to the other two. So, for starters, let's rewrite them like this:

1. Suck it up sometimes and resist other times.

2. Suck it up.

3. Quit.

Suck it up sometimes and resist other times

The first thing that needs to be said is that you already know how to do both these things. Sucking it up is just a simple matter of saying 'yes'. The past nine chapters have given you the skills necessary to resist.

If you try this dual approach, then one of two things will happen. Either your resistance will start to gain some traction or it won't. By traction, I mean that your boss will become aware that not everything can be done immediately all the time, and he or she will start to play the negotiating game with you. If this happens, then you're in business. You've managed to move them on to your territory, and you have all the skills necessary (from the previous chapters) to go forward and build a professional, relatively happy, working relationship.

If you don't start to get any traction – and I think three months or so would be adequate time within which to gauge this – then you need to give up on it. This then brings you to the other two choices.

Suck it up

By which we mean suck it up on a permanent basis, i.e. accept everything that's given to you all the time, no matter how unreasonable it is. Question 2 at the beginning of the chapter describes what will happen in these circumstances. Sooner or later, it will end in tears. Sooner or later, both parties will be unhappy, and at least one of them – you – will be deeply so. The analysis in Question 2 shows how this outcome is *guaranteed* to happen, sooner or later.

Let's state it very clearly and unequivocally. *If you choose the suck-it-up option, then you choose unhappiness.* And not just temporary unhappiness, but a permanent state that will exist as long as you remain in that job.

You *choose* it, right? Your choice. Not mine, not anybody else's. Yours. You can't blame anybody else for it. You can't blame your boss – and if you do, it won't do any good. You can't blame this book and say that the book didn't work and that you want your money back. You make the choice to be unhappy. And there – unfortunately – we must leave you. With the proviso, of course, that at any time you can reverse out of that choice and try something different. Which brings us nicely to the next section.

Quit

With this choice, you take back control of your life. You decide that unhappiness is not for you and that there must be something better waiting for you. Yes, there are risks involved – we saw some of them in the answers to

Question 3 – but you decide that these risks are worth taking. You decide to do something new – a new job, a new career, start your own business, write a novel, become a painter, learn to play the piano, or whatever. If you choose this path, then it's not just a case of throwing all the cards up in the air and seeing what happens. There are things you can do:

- Figure out what you want to do. You may feel it's too corny, it may be too Californian for your liking, but get your hands on a copy of *What Color is Your Parachute?* [1]. Work through it. Figure out what you do and don't like to do. Establish how you'd like to spend your time. Another good book to look at in this vein is *Make Money, Be Happy* [2].

- Make a plan. A plan is just a list of who's going to do what when. *Simply Brilliant* [3] will help you with making a plan if you're stuck.

- A lot of the jobs on the plan will be things that you have to do. Get stuck in and start doing them.

- Find the new thing, whatever it is.

- Walk away from the old thing.

References

1. Bolles, Richard (1999). *What Color is Your Parachute? A Practical Manual for Job-hunters and Career-changers*. Berkeley: Ten Speed Press.
2. McConnell, Carmel (2004). *Make Money, Be Happy: How to Make All the Money You Want, Doing What You Want to Do*. London: Financial Times Prentice Hall.
3. O'Connell, Fergus (2004). *Simply Brilliant*, 2nd edn. London: Financial Times Prentice Hall.

CHAPTER 11

DEALING WITH E-MAIL

If you're going to do a great job and go home on time, you're going to have to crack the problem of e-mail. This chapter tells you/reminds you how.

Q.1   You've come back from an absence and your inbox is *really* packed. There are hundreds of items in it. What should you do? (The scenario I'm imagining is one where this is a once-off rather than a regular occurrence. If it's a regular occurrence, you need to read the rest of this chapter.)

(a)   Plough through them one by one, starting with the oldest one, and deal with them.

(b)   Delete the lot and start again.

(c)   Plough through them one by one, starting with the newest one, and deal with them.

(d)   Do nothing and just let the pile continue to grow.

Q.2   Your relationship with e-mail can best be described as:

(a)   An addiction.

(b)   A master–slave relationship (with you as the slave).

(c)   A master–slave relationship (with you as the master).

(d)   Something that keeps you from doing productive work.

Q.3   Why do people expect almost instant answers to e-mails?

(a)   Because of the almost instant nature of the medium itself, i.e. you send an e-mail and almost instantly it shows up anywhere in the world.

(b) Because most people are unreasonable.

(c) Because of the nature of business in the twenty-first century.

(d) Because you've led them to believe that they'll get almost instant answers.

Answers

Q.1 (a) 1 point The point is for effort. Other than this, I think it's a daft idea.

(b) 5 points This gets my vote. It's brutal, there may be some repercussions, but – in all likelihood – all that will happen is that the important ones will get sent again. You can always claim 'We've been having technical problems' – it's the twenty-first century working person's equivalent of 'The dog ate my homework.' Also, the therapeutic value of doing this can't be over-estimated. It gives you an opportunity for a fresh start using some of the techniques in this chapter.

(c) 2 points One point for effort as in (a). However, an additional point for realizing that the more recent e-mails may make some of the older ones obsolete and so these older ones can be deleted with no repercussions whatsoever.

(d) 0 points   If I thought you were going to just let the pile grow and ignore it, I'd give you four points. In other words, this is almost as good – in my view – as answer (b). However, I think what's more likely is that you'd let the pile grow and just faff around endlessly wasting time tinkering with the pile. That's why the zero points.

Q.2   (a) 0 points   This is very serious. (I'm serious!) This chapter is about trying to cure you of this pointless dependence.

    (b) 0 points   Same answer as (a) really.

    (c) 5 points   As it should be.

    (d) 0 points   Same answer as (a) and (b).

Q.3   (a) 2 points   Probably has something to do with it.

    (b) 1 point   Maybe some people are. (Maybe everybody you deal with is!) But in general, I don't think so.

    (c) 2 points   Probably also has something to do with it.

    (d) 5 points   But this gets my vote.

Scores

15 points	If you were telling the truth – particularly with regard to Question 1 – then I salute you.
3–13 points	You have some unhealthy attitudes to this topic.
1–2 points	You really are a hard-core case, aren't you?

Maybe we humans just can't stop doing daft things. Maybe we just can't stop taking basically good ideas and making a mess out of them. Leonardo Da Vinci spent much of his life dreaming about manned flight. In the early part of the twentieth century the Wright brothers made his dream a reality. Then we went building air forces and started dropping bombs on people. We invent the internal combustion engine and motorways/freeways to drive on, which means we can travel under our own steam to many places we might not otherwise have been able to go. But what do we do? We end up with traffic jams. We invent e-mail, a method of – basically – instant communication, but what we really end up with is bringing work home with us and working longer hours.

E-mail is a good thing. No question. But overindulgence is not a good thing. And, unfortunately, too many people overindulge in e-mail. Perhaps the number-one sin is that many people have a tendency to just sit and be reactive to e-mail rather than being proactive as they would with any work task. If you do this, you'll just end up becoming a slave to e-mail. Many people are. It would not be an exaggeration to say that some people have become slaves to e-mail – they have become e-mail addicts.

Like all addictions, an addiction to e-mail can be cured. If you suffer from this addiction, this chapter will show you how to cure it. Once again, all that's missing – the elusive pixie dust – is the will to make it happen. We start with easy medicine and then up the dosage. Also, if you are really serious about this, you could measure your progress. Record how much time you spend dealing with e-mails at the moment. (Use a dance card, if you like.) Then check it again in a week or two after you've swallowed some of the medicine described below.

The medicine

The problem with most e-mail addicts is that they try to deal with every e-mail as it comes in. In essence, they try to operate an empty-at-all-times inbox. Our first job is to wean them off this habit.

So – instead of checking e-mail constantly or every time the e-mail notification goes 'Bing!', limit yourself to twice a day – once in the morning and once in the afternoon. Plan to spend no more than an hour each time, and do whatever can be done in that hour. If you can't get through all the e-mails in an hour, leave them until the next hour comes round. Also, turn off the e-mail notification on your computer.

Such a change in your behaviour is unlikely to go unnoticed for too long. Sooner or later, somebody will say to you 'Didn't you read my e-mail?' To which you should explain that you now read your e-mail only twice a day, from (say) 9 a.m. until 10 a.m. and from 2 p.m. until 3 p.m. This is useful information (not to mention a useful tip) for your colleague, and the issue should end there.

You're now ready for the next dose of medicine, which is a bit heavier.

There are two alternative treatments at this point. One would be to reduce the twice a day to once a day. However, it has to be said that hard-core e-mail junkies find this difficult to do. So, an alternative – and happily, it's even more effective – is to do the following. Twice a day, as we have described, sweep your e-mail. This time, however, rather than spending an hour on it, just deal with those ones that are 'glowing red', i.e. they are important and urgent, i.e. they *have to* be done today. Everything else, leave it. You may be tentative at first, but your confidence should grow. Finally, you should get to the point where you religiously sweep your inbox twice a day and are brutal as to what *has* to be done today. Your colleagues will probably notice that you seem to have become somewhat less tolerant of (relatively) unimportant interruptions and issues. Or, to put it another way, you deal only with things that are important.

Now, it turns out that there are even more radical things you can do. If you remember, your original philosophy essentially amounted to 'check everything that comes in, in case there's something important, and try to keep a clear inbox'. A different approach would be to say: 'If something is important enough, I need to find out about it and don't worry about the rest of the stuff in the inbox.' To implement this, you could take the following approach. Check your inbox once a day – or you could even (gasp!) go to Monday/Wednesday/Friday or even (bigger gasp!) Monday and Friday. If something is important and urgent/has to be done today/glowing red, do it. Otherwise, just leave it to rot in your inbox. Once a week, once a fortnight, once a month – the longer the interval the better, in my view – you could empty your inbox, either by going through it item by item or – better still – trash the lot and start again. Will you have missed something important? Well, why don't you do it and see what happens? If you did miss something important, you can do your inbox-sweeping more often. If you didn't, you could consider doing it even less (gasp again!) often.

CHAPTER 12

THE REST OF THE MENU

This chapter contains a bunch of other things that might help you.

Q.1   Similar scenario to Question 3 in Chapter 9. You want to start doing a great job and going home on time. There are heaps of advantages to all of your stakeholders – you, your company, your customers, your colleagues, your boss, your loved ones – if you start doing this. Of the following, which are real?

(a) It'll create a better working environment.

(b) You'll be more valued by the organization.

(c) You'll be more valued by your loved ones.

(d) Your group/team/department will be regarded more highly.

Q.2   It's early morning. You want to walk out the door at 5 p.m. today but you're already feeling guilty about it. What should you do?

(a) Nothing. It's just a natural state.

(b) Decide to be the last one to leave tomorrow to 'make up' for it.

(c) Concoct some story about a sick child/funeral/ domestic emergency, etc.

(d) Ignore the feeling.

Q.3   You want to be popular at work. Which of the following is the best way of achieving that?

(a) Do a great job and go home on time.

(b) Be part of every sports and social club outing.

(c) Always stay later than everybody else.

(d) Help your workmates.

Answers

Q.1 (a) 5 points It will – for you definitely, and your co-workers will also feel side effects (good ones!).

(b) 5 points You will.

(c) 5 points Who's to say? But maybe.

(d) 5 points They sure will – particularly if all of them were to do this.

Q.2 (a) 0 points No, it's not a natural state. Some people rarely feel guilt. Buy Mr Dyer's book [1] and read it.

(b) 0 points No. If you've done your work and delivered on your commitments, there's nothing to make up for.

(c) 0 points No. If you've done your work and delivered on your commitments, there's no need to do this either.

(d) 5 points Yep. Buy Wayne Dyer's book [2] if you think that will help.

Q.3 (a) 5 points The competent ones will love you, envy you and want to emulate you. The rest? Well, do you really care what they think?

(b) 3 points If that's what you want.

(c) 0 points And they'll love you because of what exactly?

(d) 3 points   And the best way to do that would be to have time available. And the best way to do that is what, class?

Scores

13–15 points   Easy questions again.

Anything else   Maybe the last chapter, Chapter 11, will do it for you.

You could argue that having a work/life balance is really a time-management problem; and that this book is really a time-management book dressed up in other clothes. One of the problems, though, I think, with many time-management courses and books is that they present a very prescriptive way for us to work. We are given our leather-bound loose-leaf binder with all the different forms and coloured pens. Then we are given the formula or recipe to follow. Fill in that on this form. Now break that down into these things and write them here. You can use this form in this situation. And so on.

Some people take to this like ducks to water. But, in my opinion, ways of doing time-management are as variable as there are people; and one size very definitely doesn't fit all.

You can think of this entire book as a menu of ways of doing time-management. A menu that you can choose from until you find the three–course – or six-course, or whatever number of courses you like – meal that works for you. You've seen much of the menu already. This chapter contains the rest of it.

1. Make a list of what's outstanding. This will give you focus. Then cross them off as they're done.

2. Make plans/to-do lists (yearly/monthly/weekly/daily) and update them.

3. Utilize meetings with your boss more effectively. Your choices range from keeping your head down and saying nothing to making waves and 'pushing back'. Review your workload with your manager regularly.

4. Maybe *sometimes* start early. Work lunch, work breaks, use evenings, Saturdays. But if you do this, take *at least* that much time off in lieu. Otherwise, don't even consider it.

5. Divide the day up into units of time and use these to monitor progress.

6. If you develop standards about how you manage your time, demand the same from others.

7. Challenge people's demands for your time. Be miserly with your time. Be less tolerant of people wasting your time. Charge for your time, i.e. find a way to penalize people for wasting it. Identify and penalize time-wasters, e.g. cut conversations with them. Reward those who use your time best. Don't allow other people to control your time: 'I'm in control of my time.'

8. Don't agree to every request on your time – give them alternatives.

9. Take turns regarding the venues of meetings.

10. Have appointments rather than drop-ins.

11. Have a proper meeting rather than exchanging a large number of e-mails.

12. Figure out where your time is going – record what actually happens, analyze it and come up with appropriate solutions.

13. Keep a record of what time gets wasted every day, and why. Then take steps to stop these from happening.

14. Empower others to do what you want – 'Go find out yourself!'

15. Have a good filing system.

16. Put timed standard work practices in place.

17. Keep notes on problems that you solved, and how you solved them.

18. Leave your briefcase behind. Don't take work home.

19. If you happen to work from home, I find the best thing is to behave as though you were going to a 'real' office. Get up at a set time. You may want to wash and dress as normal – though I prefer to fit that in somewhere else in the day. Arrive at your desk at a set time – even if all that means is that you clear the breakfast dishes from the kitchen table and lay out your laptop and papers. Have a list of stuff you want to get done and when it's done, stop, 'go home', you're finished for the day. Take breaks just as you would at work. Take lunch. Grab a little exercise – even if it's only a

walk to the shops. Most importantly, if you need time to clear your head of your job before you 'return' to your family or housemates, then take that time. Many people use their commute time for this, and it's actually one of the good things about commuting. (There – there had to be some benefit, didn't there?) There's nothing worse than those who share your life thinking that you're there with them when you're actually some place else.

20. Leave work when you leave work.

21. Know the resources at your disposal.

22. Be open to and give constructive criticism/suggestions.

23. Don't bite off more than you can chew. Budget your time (supply and demand).

24. Speak to your boss if you have a backlog that isn't being cleared.

25. Find the 'power hour' in the day for you.

26. Be clear and succinct in writing/talking. Write better-quality e-mails, e.g. always give an action at the end.

27. Use other people's ideas to become more effective.

28. Change people's attitude – it's all about performance, not attendance.

29. Set realistic goals/expectations with bosses/peers/customers.

30. Do a spring-clean on your computer. Have a clean-out – if you haven't referred to it in, say, a year, then throw it out.

31. Ask yourself: 'How important is this *really?*'

32. Be organized – start well. Plan your day and stick to it. Review each day to see how you did. Don't be afraid to 'push back' on your boss or get your boss to do something.

33. Book time in your calendar for yourself. Set aside time. Schedule in your private time.

34. Try not to take jobs from other people (i.e. taking the monkey from their back and putting it on to yours: try to get monkeys off your back and on to theirs).

35. Make sure people know how they stand – create the right expectations. This means you will always deliver on your commitments. If you do this, customers/bosses/peers will trust you.

36. Use teleconferencing rather than meetings

37. Take exercise. Take breaks during the day. Leave the office for breaks or for lunch. Don't go into work with a hangover – no midweek drinking. Monitor the way you sit/stand up/sit down. No alcohol at lunchtime. Eat proper food during the day. Drink more water. Get enough sleep. Take power naps. Take lunch hours/coffee breaks.

38. Fix it once.

39. Keep frequently used information to hand.

40. Keep your desk/work area tidy. Reorganize your work area.

41. Work a nine-day fortnight.

42. Be on time.

43. Escalate problems. Know escalation channels.

References

1. Dyer, Wayne (1977). *Your Erroneous Zones*. London: Michael Joseph.
2. Ibid.

CHAPTER 13

THE PERSON WHO DOES A GREAT JOB AND GOES HOME ON TIME

Yes, folks, they do exist. They're rare, but they do exist. Here's what they're like. Maybe you've met one. Maybe you know one. Hopefully by now you *are* one.

Q.1   If an organization is to become one where everybody does a great job and then goes home on time, how is that change going to happen?

(a) From the top down. The board or senior management decides, and it moves down from there.

(b) You're going to have to change the upper management's ethos.

(c) You can only do it yourself. Everybody else has to do it for themselves.

(d) The organization is never going to change.

Q.2   The approach of doing a great job and going home on time may not suit the culture of the company you work in. The culture may not encourage this approach, or it may well be antagonistic towards it. What will happen if you try to implement it for yourself?

(a) Guaranteed to succeed.

(b) Doomed to failure – not worth wasting your time on.

(c) Worth a try – company cultures do change.

(d) Could be done quietly so that you succeed but nobody would notice, so you wouldn't draw unwelcome attention to yourself.

Q.3   The approach of doing a great job and going home on time conflicts with a great truism of business – that the customer is always right. Correct?

(a) Depends on the circumstances.
(b) True.
(c) False.
(d) Don't know.

Answers

Q.1   (a) 0 points   Dream on, brother/sister!
        (b) 0 points   Good luck with that!
        (c) 5 points   Yep. And while you won't necessarily change upper management's *ethos*, you certainly will change the way they view *you*.
        (d) 0 points   Ah, come on now. Don't be so gloomy. If you've read this far and done some of the exercises, then, if nothing else, you've had some treats!

Q.2   (a) 5 points   It is actually guaranteed to succeed. If you do what we have said in the book, it will work. However, the only way you can verify that statement is to do it.
        (b) 0 points   You're wrong, you know. And what you stand to lose as a result of thinking this way is enormous.
        (c) 5 points   Sure it is – and sure they do. Company cultures change all the time.
        (d) 5 points   Well, let's clarify the answer. Yes, lots of it can be done quietly. We've given

numerous examples of ways you can do this softly softly. However, some of it can't be done quietly, and hopefully the book has prepared you for that. And will anybody notice? Yes, of course they will. And will you draw unwelcome attention to yourself. Sure, you may do. But like the salesman in Chapter 5, you'll draw the welcome attention that really counts as well.

Q.3 (a) 0 points No, it doesn't depend on the circumstances. This statement is always false. Read Chapter 6 again.

(b) 0 points No, it's not true. Read Chapter 6 again.

(c) 5 points Yes, it is false.

(d) 0 points Well, now you do.

Scores

15 points Given that we're at the end of the book, I think you're in a good frame of mind to go and fight the good fight.

10 points Still some scepticism and doubt – that's OK. Only one way to dispel them. Go and do what you have to do.

Fewer than 10 points   Go and watch the episode of *Fawlty Towers* where Basil Fawlty is sitting in his office talking to himself. Here's what he says:

'What was that?'
'That was your life, mate.'
'Do I get another one?'
'Sorry, mate.'

We've made numerous references to *Your Erroneous Zones* [1]. It's a book about how we do things that screw us up. These things, such as feeling guilty or engaging in approval-seeking, are what the author, Wayne Dyer, calls 'erroneous zones'. In the final chapter of his book, he describes a person who has managed to rid herself of such behaviour – who no longer has erroneous zones.

Being addicted to work is an erroneous zone, or rather it displays erroneous-zone behaviour. It's particularly about approval-seeking and guilt. It's about seeing yourself as a victim rather than taking control of your life.

Yet some people have shed all this behaviour. In this final chapter, I'm going to try to give you a sense of what such a person would be like. While all people may not have all the traits here, in general you'll find that many of the people who do a great job and go home on time display a lot of the following behaviours. Here we go.

Such people like coming to work. While they may not tumble out of bed in the morning singing songs from *The*

Sound of Music, once they're up and about they're ready to go and fight the good fight. Often, they go into work early to get some quiet time. Almost always, the first thing they do (or may have already done last thing the previous day) is to make a plan for the day. Part of that plan is a (prioritized) list of what they intend to get done today. But more than that, they have a sense of what is going to get done where. Where the quiet (uninterrupted, red) time will need to be so that they can get the most important things done. Where they can be a bit cooler (green) and take some interruptions or things can slide a little. Some of the things on their list will be nice-to-haves – if they don't get done, planets won't collide, share prices won't tumble, bosses won't go apoplectic. But some things will be have-to-haves, and those will be the things where our hero is going to insist on their quiet time.

Most importantly, their day will have some contingency in it. If they want to be out the door at 5 p.m., then they're going to try and be finished by 4 p.m., say. And if they are finished at 4 p.m., they have every intention of leaving. And they *will* leave. But that extra hour is the contingency. It's that time that will be used if, just as they're finished at 4 p.m., some genius comes down and says: 'I need this urgently.' If they do, then in most cases, our hero can get the thing done and still be gone by 5 p.m.

In general, on the interpersonal front, our hero tends to be calm, keeps cool and doesn't often get angry or raise their voice. If there are some interpersonal difficulties around them, they tackle them as soon as possible rather than letting them fester. But in general, such people are involved in such things less often than most. This is primarily because, in doing a great job, they are pretty much always delivering on their commitments and so generate a lot less work-related stress as a result.

One of the traits that's almost always noted about people who do a great job and go home on time is how they are regarded by those around them. I've heard it described in a number of ways, but perhaps the most vivid are these two: 'They don't take any crap from the management.' 'They tell it like it is.' Not for them to be told: 'We have to do this, we have no choice.' Others may engage in such delusional behaviour, but not our hero. He or she tells it like it is, identifies the possible alternative ways forward and then lets the greater-minds-than-ours decide. If they (the powers that be) choose to engage in further delusional behaviour, than our hero gently but firmly drags them back to reality.

When you try to hand some task to our hero, it's not a trouble-free process. This is true no matter how senior you are in the organization. Our hero will never just accept something just because it's been lobbed over the wall. They may know straight away how long something is going to take. Then they will tell you that – irrespective of whether that's what you wanted to hear. On the other hand, they may have to go and investigate it – do some estimates, build a plan. In that case, they will tell you when they'll know how long it's going to take. You can exert all the pressure in the world, you can do the Chicken Licken sky-is-falling thing. They won't bat an eyelid. That's your problem. Theirs is to look at what they've been handed, and they will do that to the best of their ability.

Our hero is challenged by their job. They are interested in it and see a value in what they're doing. They have a positive attitude and are upbeat. This is true even if they're not trying to put someone on the moon. The challenge comes from the fact that they have had the conversation with the boss about what would be the best possible performance that they could deliver. Our hero knows where the bar is, and when they get to the point where they can routinely clear it they work with their boss and stakeholders to raise the bar.

Our hero has a good relationship with their boss. By this, I don't mean that it's friendly or even cordial. But it is professional. The boss understands what our hero expects from them because our hero has told them! Our hero delivers a you-can-take-it-to-the-bank level of service to the boss. By this, I mean that when our hero makes a commitment, his or her boss can depend on it. What boss would not be happy with such service? Our hero maybe has more one-on-ones with his or her boss than do most other people. These are not about sucking up to the boss. Rather, they are about making sure that both parties are – in a constantly changing world – absolutely in sync about objectives and their priorities.

When it comes to dealing with interruptions, you'll again find that our hero is very different from run-of-the-mill people. First, you'd better think carefully before you go and interrupt them. If you have a question or a problem for them, it better be stated clearly and well thought out. You'd better have RTFM'd (Read the Blessed Manual) and tried to figure it out for yourself. Otherwise, they'll give you short shrift. Depending on their personality, they may be very brusque or very polite. Or they may approach it another way. They may insist on you being specific about the problem by getting you to write it down or filling out a form. But if you haven't done your preparation, you'll be left in little doubt that you shouldn't have come to them.

Think twice as well before you approach them for a 'Did you see the match last night?' conversation. If they're in their red time, you'll make little headway. You'll be dismissed – maybe courteously, maybe not. And don't even *dream* of approaching them with a last-minute emergency. They invented the 'Your lack of planning is not my emergency' school of dealing with crises. They may do you a favour and save your bacon, but it will be just that. Don't bank on it happening every time, because it won't. And be grateful for the times when it does. And for goodness' sake, try and learn something from it, and do things differently next time.

Even if you're not in any of the preceding categories, your interruption may still not get through. They have one last way to keep you at bay. They may say: 'Take a ticket'; i.e. they can't deal with you now, but they have a slot for you at 3.30 p.m.

Our hero makes it a rule to almost never say 'yes' straight up. They have numerous tricks that don't make you feel like they have said 'no' to you – even though they have. One of their favourites is to double or treble the amount of time you give them for the deadline. So, for example, it's Monday at 11 a.m. and you come scampering along to them and say: 'I need this by lunchtime [1 p.m.] today', essentially giving them a two-hour deadline. Unfazed by this, they'll reply: 'Impossible. I could have it done by the end of the day [5 p.m.] though.' The request for a two-hour turnaround has been met with a five-hour [11–1 and 2–5] response. This may be the end of it or it may just be their opening position. But you certainly didn't get a 'yes'.

In general, people who do a great job and go home on time like their jobs. They may not be going 'woopee-doo' as they drag themselves out of bed every day, but they do seem to have higher than average energy levels. By and large, they are content with things at work. They realize that they are not victims at work. Rather they can – to a large extent – choose how they want things to be, and then negotiate that with the powers that be. If the powers that be don't or won't play ball, then our hero will find some place where they will.

Our hero is free from guilt and certainly doesn't feel guilty when they walk out the door every day at 5 p.m. Neither do they worry particularly about work once they've left it. They do a great job and go home on time; and when they leave work, they leave work. There's a whole other day tomorrow to get stuck into things again.

Neither do they engage in approval-seeking. Their work speaks for itself. It makes its own statement and any other comment or statement is superfluous. As the Roman philosopher Sallust said: 'When the facts are at hand, what's the need for words?'

Often, people who do a great job and go home on time are good-humoured – though I have come across exceptions, particularly in the software industry! It's all related to the confidence they have in their ability to do their job and get a result. A corollary of this is that they don't blame others or, rather, they don't try to absolve themselves of responsibility. If they screw up, they say so and take whatever fallout that comes as a result. A further corollary of this is that they are not afraid to fail or take risks.

And if all this sounds too amazing to be true, then it's important to remember that it's not something that is outside your control. You too can be like this – irrespective of the boss, company, culture, industry sector or anything else you find yourself in. It's not something that might happen to you given the right set of circumstances. It's a decision; a decision that you and only you can make. You can make that decision today – if you want to.

References

1. Dyer, Wayne (1977). *Your Erroneous Zones*. London: Michael Joseph.

Afterword

In one sense, none of this is particularly difficult. The techniques described in the preceding chapters could hardly be described as rocket science. You don't need a university degree or a postgraduate qualification to understand or apply them. They are not propositions from Wittgenstein.

Yet in a very real sense, what this book is encouraging you to do is the hardest thing in the world. This book is encouraging you to make changes to your own behaviour. There are all the obvious benefits that we have seen. But these may not be enough.

It's a cliché that life is not a rehearsal, but it's not. What is at stake is you, your life, your happiness and the happiness of those you love. The stakes could hardly be higher. But even these stakes may not be enough to make you want to change.

I hope for your sake that they are.

And finally – change isn't easy. If you think it will help, send me an e-mail at: fergus.oconnell@etpint.com and I'll send you reminders to try to keep you on the straight and narrow.

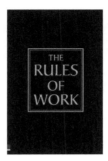

brilliant CV
second edition

Jim Bright

0273702114

April 2005

Brilliant is an international bestseller and the UK's bestselling CV book. It remains the only CV book to be based on actual research into what employers and recruiters want to see. Now the fully updated and revised second edition reveals three new chapters and all the latest research. The number one CV guide has just got better!

brilliant interview
second edition

Ros Jay

0273703560

May 2005

What do interviewers really want from a candidate? How do they decide whether to hire you or someone else? Who better to advise interviewees than interviewers? Arm yourself with the advantage of knowing what interviewers are looking for and how to supply it.

Like Brilliant this book is highly practical and interactive, with features such as tips from the experts, shining examples, horror stories, questions and quizzes to get you thinking. Learn to show yourself in the best possible light and maximise your chances of getting the job.

Guaranteed to propel you into your dream job!

The Brilliant series is the number one job-hunting series, based on actual research into what recruiters are really looking for

If you wish to find out more about any of these titles or view our full list visit us at:
www.pearson-books.com